The ACCIDENTAL FARMER
The Story of Ross Farm

JOAN WATSON *with* MURRAY CREED

Nimbus Publishing Limited
3731 Mackintosh St, Halifax, NS, B3K 5A5
(902) 455-4286 nimbus.ca
Printed and bound in Canada

NB1324

Cover photo: Ernest Cadegan
Interior layout: Grace Laemmler
Cover Design: Jenn Embree

Library and Archives Canada Cataloguing in Publication

Watson, Joan, 1932-, author
The accidental farmer : the story of Ross Farm / Joan Watson with Murray Creed.

(Stories of our past)
Includes bibliographical references and index.
Issued in print and electronic formats.
ISBN 978-1-77108-527-4 (softcover).—ISBN 978-1-77108-528-1 (PDF)

1. Ross Farm Museum—Juvenile literature. 2. Ross family—Museums—Nova Scotia—New Ross—Juvenile literature. 3. Ross family—Juvenile literature. 4. Historic farms—Nova Scotia—New Ross—Juvenile literature. 5. Agricultural museums—Nova Scotia—New Ross—Juvenile literature. 6. Agriculture—Nova Scotia—History—Juvenile literature. 7. Farm life—Nova Scotia—History—Juvenile literature. 8. Frontier and pioneer life—Nova Scotia—Juvenile literature. 9. New Ross (N.S.)—History—Juvenile literature. I. Creed, Murray, author II. Title. III. Series: Stories of our past (Halifax, N.S.)

S548.6.C2W38 2017 j630.74716'23 C2017-904115-0
C2017-904116-9

NOVA SCOTIA

Nimbus Publishing acknowledges the financial support for its publishing activities from the Government of Canada, the Canada Council for the Arts, and from the Province of Nova Scotia. We are pleased to work in partnership with the Province of Nova Scotia to develop and promote our creative industries for the benefit of all Nova Scotians.

DEDICATED TO

Mary Ross, Nina White, and the women of Ross Farm

Animals are a charming attraction at Ross Farm, a living farm musem in rural Nova Scotia that takes visitors back in time. (MATTHEW GATES)

CONTENTS

Employees at Ross Farm dress in period costumes designed and made at the museum, which welcomed its millioneth visitor in 2010. (MATTHEW GATES)

FOREWORD

I HEARD MANY STORIES OF courage, hardship, and hope when I was growing up in Rosebank Cottage, the house that my great-great-grandfather Captain William Ross built two hundred years ago. Just after the War of 1812, Captain Ross led disbanded soldiers through the woods to settle an area which is now known as New Ross where he and his wife, Mary, pioneered the farm which is now Ross Farm Museum and where I now have the honour of chairing the board of trustees.

I have always felt that the fantastic story must be told of this young couple from Cork, Ireland, who braved four Atlantic voyages on sailing ships, were shipwrecked twice, and raised six children born in primitive conditions on three continents. William died at thirty-nine, leaving Mary to raise a daughter and five sons and keep the farm going until their generation could take over.

The idea of producing this book came about from many conversations with Joan Watson while driving to and from board of trustees meetings in New Ross. Joan agreed that this true tale needed telling and that the woman's role was often neither recorded nor appreciated. She wanted to demonstrate the strength, courage, and versatility of women who supported their husbands down through the years—women like the origional Mary Ross and my mother, Nina White, who was the last operator of Ross Farm and, after the early death of my father, Mark, arranged for it to become Canada's only living farm museum.

The challenge of writing this book was taken on by Joan and her husband, Murray Creed. They spent countless hours researching and writing *The Accidental Farmer*. It has become a labour of love.

Joan Watson is herself a strong woman and demonstrated throughout her life and career as host of CBC's *Marketplace* and many other initiatives that no challenge is too big. Thank you, Joan. I am proud of you and of this book—a legacy that will live on and bring important history and enjoyment for all age groups for years to come.

Valerie White
Descendant of William and Mary Ross

A visit to Ross Farm Museum can be magical thanks to the friendly staff and animals. (MATTHEW GATES)

INTRODUCTION

AGRICULTURE HAS ALWAYS HAD A grip on me. Grandpa's Annapolis Valley apple orchard was a renewable resource, reliably pink and white in spring and rosy red every autumn—best seen when hanging upside down from a rubber tire swing. In this position I would choose the first apple of autumn.

In grade eight, an appendectomy provided a respite from lessons and a chance to binge on neglected books. That was not the way my father saw it, however; outdoor activity would help the healing. He owned a vacant lot next door to our city house. He plowed it up, fertilized the clay soil, and gifted me with ten dozen tomato plants and the direction that they be set out immediately and watered.

I planted all 120 of them, turned on the hose, and left, and when I returned it was to see the rear view of my six-foot-two father hands on hips, his feet firmly planted in mud. Only the tips of the plants could be seen.

I had mixed emotions as one by one, encouraged by the sun, they lifted their leaves and chose life over death. They blossomed and produced endlessly. The first tomato I ate. The first basket I took to the kitchen. From then on it was a frantic rush through July and August to pick and sell mounds of tomatoes to the local grocer. My commission was 10 percent of sales, handed back to me after my father checked my bookkeeping.

By September, I felt as squashed as the tomatoes I stepped on.

Salvation arrived the day the circus came to town. The bigwig operators, driving dented Caddies, parked with their exhaust pipes directed a foot away from the tomato patch. They always held confabs in the cars with the engines running. The black emissions and heat made short work of my crop. When the police arrived after reports of crooked dealings at the fair, they found me in a heated confrontation with the perpetrators. When the police were through with them, the last car drove out through the tomato patch.

My association with agriculture continued when I joined CBC as a farm broadcaster. It was mandatory to enter a plowing competition for the press at the International Plowing Match in Guelph, Ontario. I practised by plowing up half of Halton County, Ontario, with a borrowed tractor and three-furrow plow. On competition day, it rained and my wet wool sweater smelled. I took off for home. While soaking in the tub, the phone rang. When the plowing was finished, I had succeeded in beating my male colleagues by covering every blade of grass in my furrows. I have the trophy now, even though it turned as black as the dead tomato plants.

The daughter of an "Aggie" from the Nova Scotia Agricultural College, I married another agriculturalist from Macdonald College, Quebec, only after being assured that I would not be expected to plow fields or pick tomatoes.

Today, the attraction for me at Ross Farm Museum is the commitment to demonstrate to schoolchildren and all visitors the relevance of farming in our lives today.

Old ways change in the light of new knowledge, but there is much to be learned from early days. Mechanization, factory farming, marketing boards, and trade agreements all have impact on the food we eat today and distance us from the source of our food. This accounts for the popularity of farm markets and their emphasis on pesticide-free food and other good things.

Getting back to our roots also accounts for the popularity of Ross Farm Museum, where today's generation can become acquainted with traditional farming and with beautiful, humanely treated farm animals. Children can explore, experiment, and learn from the knowledgeable staff who delight in surprising and engaging kids in a way that complements their school curriculum. The museum, which opened in 1970, is Canada's only working farm museum where visitors can see and experience authentic nineteenth- and twentieth-century farm life. Open year-round, the museum has averaged twenty-five thousand visitors a year, including hundreds of school classes; it passed the one million mark in 2010.

Ross Farm's connection with educators and organizations that "think green" will continue to influence what the farm offers in its new Learning Centre as pioneering on Ross Farm continues to offer new miracles in agriculture. There's a soft spot in my heart for our yearly Pumpkin Planting Day for school kids. It takes spectacular faith to plant a small seed in the ground and expect anything to happen, somewhat like planting a small wilting tomato plant and expecting an abundance of juicy fruit. But the kids all come back in autumn and find at their numbered stakes their perfect pumpkin. One look at their faces tells it all. It doesn't matter whether it's a tomato or a pumpkin, a seed or the germ of a new idea, new growth yields a ripe reward.

MOMENTS IN TIME

This story is a series of events—moments, some sad, some happy, moments of terror, moments of bravery. In this narrative we have tried to capture moments in time, moments of place, moments of chance, and moments of fate.

Some episodes are based strictly on fact. We know exactly what happened, how and why, as accurately as could be expected after two centuries have elapsed; others are based on known events, of which the details are lacking, while others are moments that could have happened given the circumstance and the tenor of the times. All of the moments in this book are real. We invite you to share in the saga of William and Mary Ross and their founding of what was to become Ross Farm Museum.

Visitors, especially children, are delighted by the many animals. Ross Farm is known for its heritage breeds, introduced in 1990. (ROSS FARM)

In the early days of Ross Farm Museum, considerable research into the family backgrounds of William and Mary Ross was initiated by Ron Barkhouse, first president of the museum, who commissioned researchers to peruse British and Irish records now in the files of New Ross Historical Society.

In the late 1900s, Joan Waldron of the Nova Scotia Museum visited Belfast, Dublin, and Cork in Ireland, and Bedfordshire, Kew, and London in England. She conducted research at the Bedfordshire Public Archives, the National Registry of Archives in London, and the Public Record Office at Kew. She searched the Belfast Public Record Office, the National Library in Dublin, and the Cork Archives and Library. Many of the scenes in this book are based on her research and conclusions.

This we know: William Ross Sr., who married Jane Keys in 1764, was a prosperous owner and operator of a watch- and clock-making enterprise on upscale Grand Parade in Cork, Ireland, at the beginning of the nineteenth century. In the days before the factory manufacture of timepieces, a watchmaker was the high-tech artisan of the time. William Sr. also owned a dozen other properties, revealed in recorded deed transfers. His son William was the heir apparent, as the older son, John, had moved to Chile. William had three sisters, Catherine, Maria, and Percale. It is thought that the Ross family was of Scottish origin.

Nothing is known of the family history of Mary Williams. Paul O'Regan of the Cork City Library, Grand Parade, informed us that birth, baptism, and death records of St. Peter's Anglican Church, where the Williams family worshipped, were moved to Dublin for safekeeping, but unfortunately were destroyed in the Irish Rebellion of 1798.

Custom suggests that Mary's family would be of the same social class as that of William's, as it was the norm then to marry within one's social strata. It was also the custom for the suitor to ask the father for his daughter's hand in marriage.

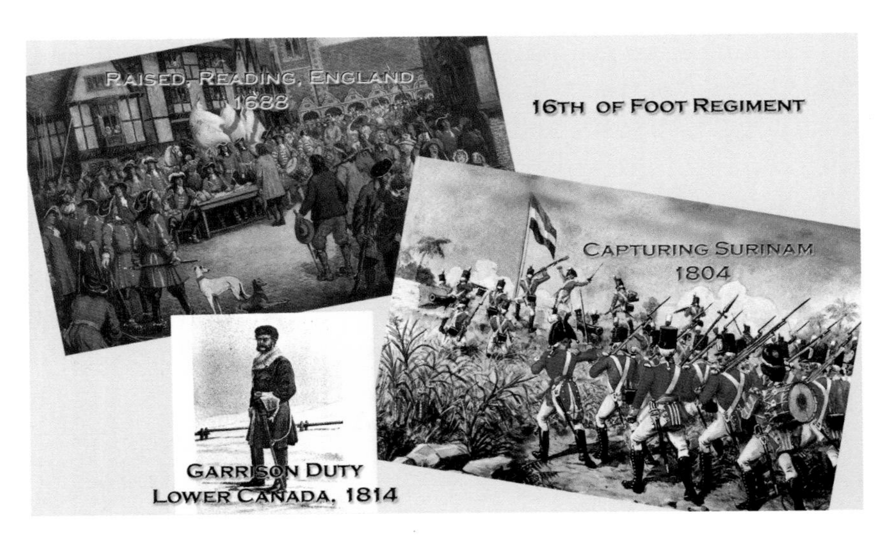

After William joined the British Army, he was sent to Surinam to help defend the South American colony from future attacks. (MURRAY CREED GRAPHIC)

CHAPTER 1

IN HIS MAJESTY'S SERVICE: SOUTH AMERICA

MARY WILLIAMS STOOD OUTSIDE HER father's library door trying to catch a word, a phrase, a clue to the lively conversation going on behind the big oak door.

Her father's approval was considered essential.

Mary had little to worry about. William Ross of Cork was a fine catch, a university graduate, the son of prosperity. He could offer his bride position and wealth at a time when half of Ireland was starving. Life with William would be comfortable, safe, and prosperous.

It was a family expectation that William would succeed his father in business on the Grand Parade and eventually inherit the shop, family home, and extensive real estate. Mary's feelings for William were genuine and deep. She wanted their children, boys and girls, to be well educated and raised in a secure home with sufficient income.

Finally, the two men came out arm in arm, looking well pleased. Beaming, William assured her that they would prosper together.

William looked at the pocket watch his father had made to mark his graduation and reminded Mary that they were expected for dinner at his family home. This would be an opportunity for William to tell his mother and father that they had received Mary's father's blessing to marry.

There was a festive air at dinner. There were two toasts, one for

This wedding dress (left) was the fashion of the day when Mary Williams married William Ross. She would have worn something similar. (MURRAY CREED GRAPHIC)

William's newly won university degree and a second for the young couple's engagement. There were diamond earrings for Mary and £500 for William.

But wait, William's mind was not fully on toasts and good wishes. He was preoccupied with another announcement he wanted to make—how to tell his family and Mary of a development that

was sure to be taken as exceedingly bad news. He planned to join the British Army.

William had no intention of becoming a clockmaker and every intention of joining the army and going to war. Britain was fighting on almost every continent.

There was no way to break the news gently, so William suddenly jumped into the conversation with: "Every young man has a duty to fight for his country, and that includes me."

Unwittingly, the education William's father had provided had also made his son highly qualified for a commission in the army. It would cost his father £400 for a commission as ensign plus another £200 for uniform and sword, which William didn't mention. Speechless best describes the family's reaction.

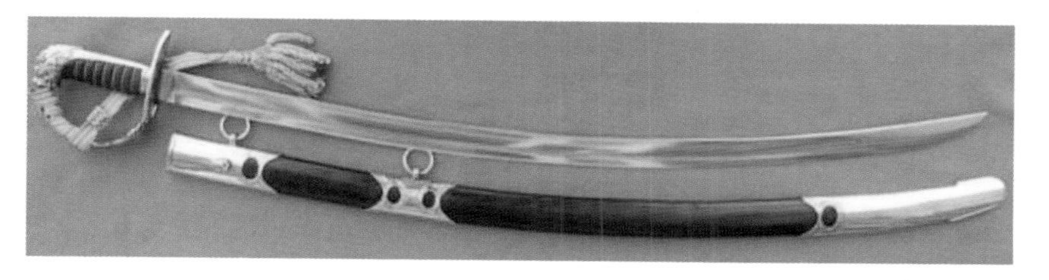

William's military uniform included an officer's sword similar to this. The swords were considered a mark of rank. (MURRAY CREED GRAPHIC)

The little hand-carved cuckoo clock on the dining room wall had the last word and repeated its opinion ten times: "Cuckoo!"

As William walked Mary home after dinner, she hardly knew what to say and so said nothing. Had he known that Mary was now rethinking the whole idea of marrying him, he might have sobered up in a hurry. He might have realized Mary's expectations had been scuttled: the promise of the family home, the security that would come with inheriting the clockmaker's shop, the proximity of family and friends, and the benefits of providing first-class schooling for their children. Every dream dashed.

Mary felt disheartened. Nevertheless, slowly, she accepted a new role: William would lead and Mary would follow. They were married in 1805 at St. Peter's, an old Anglican stone church in Cork.

CLOCKS - THE TRADITION

William's father's clock- and watchmaking business would have been an important part of upper-class Cork life. One of his products would have been the long-case clock, which, thanks to an American songwriter, would become known as the grandfather clock.

In watching its pendulum swing to and fro,
Many hours had he spent while a boy;
And in childhood and manhood the clock seemed to know
And to share both his grief and his joy.
For it struck twenty-four when he entered at the door,
With a blooming and beautiful bride;
But it stopped short — never to go again —
When the old man died.

"Grandfather clocks" didn't get that name until 1876, when Henry Work published a song called "Grandfather's Clock," a poignant ditty about the intertwined lives of a clock and a man, inspired by the legend of the long-case clock at the George Hotel in North Yorkshire, England.

Very few people in late-eighteenth-century America had clocks, and in the early 1800s, only the very wealthy could afford them—they cost around seventy dollars: more than a year's salary for most people. During William's short lifetime, clocks became much cheaper and more people were able to afford them. By around 1850, clocks cost as little as two dollars and every household would have one.

Early in 1805, William wrote to the Duke of York, commander of the British Army, requesting a commission as ensign, the lowest officer rank. It was granted in September; he was attached to the 16th Regiment of Foot and posted to its training base at Reading, near London.

On September 30, 1806, William and Mary's first child was born—their only girl. They named her Mary. She would prove to have her mother's admirable qualities of loyalty and courage.

At their next family dinner in Cork, William was resplendent in his full dress officer's uniform: black top hat six inches high, red tunic coat with silver facings, yellow flashings on the collar, white trousers, black leather leggings, white stockings, black patent-leather shoes, and white lace shirt. Mary detected a certain swagger that William adopted when in full dress.

Everything in Mary's life now hinged on William's postings, perhaps to be shipped to the continent to fight in the Napoleonic War. No, he was promoted to lieutenant in March 1807 and shortly after posted to steamy Surinam in South America. The British had just captured the colony from the Dutch, and it had to be defended.

In general terms, Mary's role was to follow her husband to battlefields and garrison duty around the world and to bear and rear their children in primitive conditions, often under fire. It is doubtful William made any mention of tropical diseases, deadly snakes, poisonous arrows, or hair-raising sea travels.

Mary could foresee the impossibility of caring for and protecting her toddler on rough winter seas in confined quarters without warmth, milk, or fresh food. The thought of giving up her baby was painful. However, more painful still would be losing her daughter to the dangers of the jungle or warfare. William's parents were more than willing to care for her.

Mary now realized that any of their future children would certainly be born into a dangerous existence. A permanent home and a first-rate education would be denied them.

Mary had no choice other than to turn to immediate matters—packing. She was allowed two small trunks for all their clothing, bedding, and personal effects. Accustomed to plenty of fine Irish linen, it was hard to be limited to one sheet, a blanket, two towels, sanitary supplies, soap, candles, diapers. Mary allowed herself three luxuries: one book, *Robinson Crusoe*, one tin of English biscuits, and a piece of needlework (a cottage surrounded by roses). She chose the thread carefully, added needles and notions. This little luxury saved her sanity during the loneliness she would suffer. Mary judged everything with one thought in mind: was it essential?

She added medicines, bandages, and disinfectant, a kitchen knife and scissors, and mosquito netting. With regret, she put her fine dresses back in the closet. She purchased a rough serge coat, a shawl, boots instead of slippers, and heavy pants instead of skirts (she had never worn trousers), undergarments, and stockings. She slammed the lid. When the day of departure came, they would board the little vessel known as the packet and sail from Cork to Liverpool to board a larger sailing ship for the ocean journey. The day of parting, family, friends, and neighbours saw them off at the Cork waterfront. The baby clung to Mary, sensing her anxiety. The family embraced, took the baby, turned, and left. Mary outstretched her hand to the now retreating figures, said an unheard "goodbye."

William and Mary had grown up in troubled times. They were in their teens when Napoleon Bonaparte began the rampage that shook Europe and spread worldwide. Word of victories and defeats filtered back slowly in those days before today's electronics.

Lord Nelson's victory at the Battle of Trafalgar in 1805 destroyed Napoleon's plans to invade England, and Lord Wellington's win at Waterloo in October in 1815, which stopped Bonaparte in his tracks, was still to come.

Less dramatic but equally essential was garrison duty—that unsung, boring job of guarding the forts that controlled waterways, other strategic locations, and battle lines.

WINTER VOYAGE TO SURINAM

William and Mary stood on the crowded wharf in Liverpool that cold January morning in 1808, en route to South America. Liverpool was at that time one of England's busiest ports, a hub on the Middle Passage trade triangle. Hundreds of sailing ships carried manufactured goods to West Africa. Those goods were traded for slaves to be shipped to America, to trade for sugar to be offloaded back in Liverpool. The Liverpool docks were just a short walk down from where The Beatles would live, sing, and record a century and a half later.

One of these ships had been converted to a troopship and lay alongside taking on army supplies and personnel. Those were dangerous times—the Napoleonic Wars were raging and cargo ships were ready prizes for opposing navies.

As their square-rigger ship loaded for the Atlantic voyage to Barbados, Mary's mood turned to apprehension.

The scene was chaotic: piles of gear, equipment, and foodstuff, hundreds of soldiers burdened with kit bags. Animals. As the troops filed slowly up the gangplank, Mary noticed that their coats were inside out. "That's to keep their uniforms clean," William told her. "It's dirty down in the hold." Overrun with rats and slippery with slops, "filthy" would have been a more accurate description. More disturbing was the sight of a group of women and children pushed to one side on the wharf. Who were they?

They were the families of soldiers who had boarded the ship. Of the hundreds huddled on the wharf, only four families would be allowed to board. They would take part in a "lucky" draw from slips of paper in William's hat. Most would read "no go." Only four would say "go."

Each woman in turn stepped up and took a small square, sealing her fate. The four winning scraps of paper were drawn and the frantic losers—young women and babies— were pushed aside. Now rejected, they faced separation from their lovers and husbands for years. They huddled on the cobblestones with no food, no lodgings, and watched as the four "lucky" women and their children were allowed on board to join their husbands below, to share one of the narrow bunks, banked four high, with half rations for wives and one-quarter rations for children. This brutal system was instituted by the British in the eighteenth century and continued until well into the next. Mary, as the wife of an officer, was spared the lottery. She and her lieutenant husband would share a six-foot-square cabin on the quarterdeck with a bunk and barely enough room to stand up to dress. Mary's earlier apprehension returned. She didn't like the sea.

Mary had left more behind than their first-born child, the only daughter she would ever bear. She had also left the only security she would ever know. She now saw the venture as a dangerous sea voyage to a God-forsaken tropical outpost ridden with disease, dangerous snakes, and a hostile enemy. William saw it as an exciting experience. They were both right.

The ship came alive. Men went aloft. Bow lines and stern lines were hauled aboard, coiled, and stowed below for the six-to-eight-week voyage, and the ship slowly slipped into the powerful Mersey's thirty-foot outgoing tide, which swept it out to sea.

Liverpool slipped astern. An hour later, they cleared the river and set course southward into the Irish Sea. William and Mary stood on deck, looking out toward the misty coast of Ireland. The ship passed Tuskar Rock; that murderous outcropping that had claimed so many ships was of no concern to William and Mary now. Four years later, on their return voyage, it would be. As night fell, the rocky coast of Ireland became a memory, replaced by the heaving grey seas of the wintery North Atlantic.

Next morning they cleared the English Channel and sailed into the open Atlantic with a twenty-knot northwest wind and a following sea. The rigging strained and the masts, spars, and hull creaked and groaned. To Mary's untrained ears the ship sounded to be in misery. To a seasoned sailor it was a comforting noise, caused

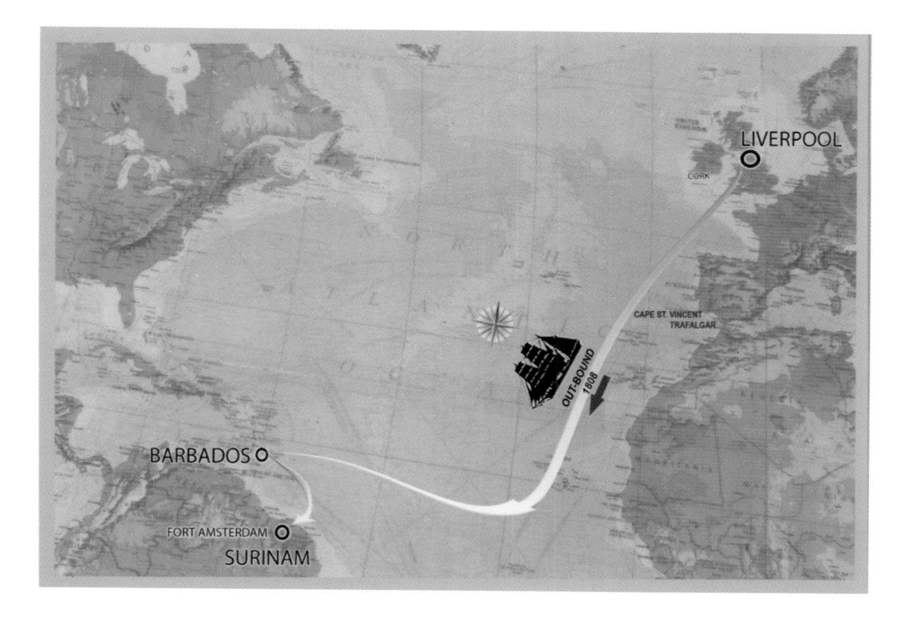

Mary and William made the voyage to South America from Liverpool following this route. (MURRAY CREED GRAPHIC)

by the give and take of seasoned wood that allowed the planks to absorb some of the motion. With each roll and pitch of the ship, seams opened and closed, salt water seeped in and flooded the bilge. A few of the troops were ordered by William to help operate the pumps in the continuous battle against the sea, providing welcome relief for the ship's crew busy on deck and aloft.

If the creaking stops, the ship is doomed, sailors say. "Only rotten wood is silent, already dead and destined for the bottom."

Mary's practical mind could accept her husband's reassuring words until in a rough sea the squeaking and groaning became so loud it reminded her of the sounds that used to come from a slaughterhouse at the end of the road at home

This ship was never quiet. Thundering feet, yells, bells, and crashing seas left Mary standing, swaying, slowly making her way to the only place to sit, their bunk.

Their three-masted, square-rigged ship called a West Indiaman was the workhorse of the Atlantic. These rough-and-ready cargo ships plied between Liverpool, England, and Bridgetown, Barbados, in all weather, year-round. Some had been slave ships, hauling thousands of black captives from Africa to Liverpool for transshipment to America. Some of the ships were chartered by the British army to move troops and supplies to Caribbean and South American postings.

The ship rolled violently in the thirty-knot wind, as twenty-foot waves slammed against the port side and green seas swept the deck.

In the dark hold, the troops and the four women and their children huddled in bunks, bracing themselves against the pitch and yaw of the ship. The stink of riled-up bilge water filled the air. The women who had "won" the lottery must have known by then that they were the losers.

Mary lay seasick in their humid cabin while William stood on the afterdeck bracing against the roll and pitch, salt spray drenching his face, enjoying it all.

He was excited, in his element from the time the square-rigger met the open sea. Most landsmen are seasick first night out. Not William. He marvelled at the force as the fierce gale drove the West Indiaman through the seas. He had never seen or felt anything like it.

Growing up in Cork with its military and naval tradition and its world-trading seaport, William's taste for travel and adventure had developed as he read Sir Francis Drake, Ferdinand Magellan, Jacques Cartier, Leif Ericsson, and Benjamin Franklin. He was delighted that their course would take them past Trafalgar, where Horatio Nelson had put Napoleon's fleet to shame three years earlier and forestalled his invasion of England.

William had studied the writings of Henry the Navigator. This voyage would take him past Sagres on the tip of Portugal where the principles of navigation at sea were developed.

Navigational equipment was unsophisticated at the time Mary and William crossed the Atlantic on a rough cargo ship. Crews relied on tools such as sextants, compasses, and maps. (MURRAY CREED GRAPHIC)

Mary awoke to more noise, a wildly swinging lantern overhead. She rose and looked out at the sky. A dark hulking mass of cloud seething and rolling over itself was bearing down on the vessel. Nevertheless, Mary stepped out for fresh air during a brief lull in the storm. She found herself wholly exposed to sea and wind. In her attempt to get to the rail to throw up, tiny particles of ice with the sting of needles blinded her.

Carried beyond the handhold, Mary gasped and struggled for breath as a wave running the length of the deck whipped her feet out from under her. As she was swept several yards, almost to the stern, a seaman collared her and turned her over to William. He was in a state of fury, something she had never seen before. As he manhandled her back to the cabin, he shouted over the storm: "Get in there and stay there!"

Shaken by sobs and fear, she lay on the sodden boards, and for the first time she gave in to a sense of helplessness and wept. She wept for the daughter left in Cork; she wept for the arms of her mother. Finally she slept.

As the days passed, the boredom didn't. The needlepoint was finished. Mary debated picking it apart and doing it again. However, she looked at each small flaw in the canvas as a marker of the passing days. She remembered finishing the small rose, stitched in pink until her thread ran out. The last petal was now an uncommonly deep red.

The cottage with a slightly crooked roofline had a staunch little chimney, the way she imagined her first home would be. Where it would be was unknown. Mary, not for the first time, wondered if their journeying would ever lead to a hearthside. She cautioned herself to stop dreaming and to make the best of it. William, about to go on deck, paused. "You'll get your cottage, Mary." Mary contemplated the knotholes in the wooden wall. She imagined the eyes of small woodland animals looking back at her. Two close-set holes and a crack in the wood suggested the face of a man she dubbed "Lutine." Many small and large frustrations were vented at Mr. Lutine, sparing William.

Mary felt seasick and the confinement of the cabin made it worse, so in spite of William's warning, she ventured out on deck again. Staring at the grey waves while on deck she had a sudden and unbidden sense of panic. How deep is the water? What swims below: sharks, whales, and unknown creatures? How far down to the bottom? For the first time, her fear of the sea became real. The vessel that looked large, solid, and trustworthy at dockside now appeared to be a creaking concoction of timbers and canvas unsuited to sail through the elements.

Mary turned quickly and went back to the cabin where the warm light of the oil lamp gave some comfort.

Much later William came back exhausted and flopped on the straw mattress. Mary crawled into the narrow bunk with him, hoping for comfort. William was asleep.

Perhaps this art, found hanging in the cottage that Mary and William eventually inhabited, resembled the cottage that Mary dreamed of during that long voyage. The artwork, in poor condition when found, has been attributed to Willam. (BOB HUTT)

Below decks, the few women on board had become accustomed to the lack of privacy. They went about their intimacies with the men they had accompanied without the benefit of cover. Privies were open and crude, just buckets to be dumped over the side later, hopefully downwind. By comparison, Mary and William were well off.

After three weeks, the last fresh food was gone, and the meals had become repetitious and consistently bad. William and Mary ate everything on the tin plate they shared, with a few exceptions. William, lost in thought, looked serious. Mary, watching, suddenly saw something move on the plate they shared and said: "Do you want the cockroach, or shall I eat it?" He laughed.

SHIPBOARD RATIONS

Daily ration totalled about three pounds, including biscuit, meat, dried peas, oatmeal, butter, and cheese. Meat came in barrels, pickled in brine, often with more than a fair proportion of extra gristle and bone thrown in by suppliers, knowing that by the time the barrel was opened the ship would be hundreds of miles out to sea. Biscuit was rock-hard bread, often infested with weevils. Butter went rancid and cheese became dry and mouldy. Duff was a gooey mixture of flour, suet, salt, and water boiled in a sail-cloth bag. If the cook added raisins and sugar, the dish was called Spotted Dog.

- Monday – cheese and duff
- Tuesday – two pounds of salt beef
- Wednesday – dried peas and duff
- Thursday – one pound of salt pork
- Friday – dried peas and cheese
- Saturday – two pounds of salt beef

THE TRADE WINDS

The ship's outbound course carried her south to the coast of Africa where she caught the Sahara-born trade winds west across the Atlantic to Barbados.

Mary and William were now in the tropics. Sailor lore has it that when butter melts on the plate, it's time to change from a southerly course to a westerly one. The skies cleared and the winter cold was slowly replaced by tropical heat as the weary soldiers and their wives, in groups of a dozen, ventured on deck, glad to be free of the miserable hold. They felt a change of air—the trade winds.

Mary, basking in the warmth on deck, slept, and woke feeling a trace of sunburn on her face.

The ship's carpenter drove two brass nails in the deck, twelve yards apart. Rolls of duck cloth were measured out in twelve-yard lengths and served to each man with needles and thread.

The soldiers set out to sew hot-weather tops, trousers, and broad-brimmed hats to replace their heavy uniforms. Can't you image the comments on deck when the troops modelled their new clothes?

Forty-five days, and the long voyage would soon be over.

Flying fish began to land on deck; others skimmed over the waves like super-sized iridescent hummingbirds. The young soldiers scrambled to catch them, the first fresh food in weeks. There would be a taste for supper, fried in rancid butter, true, but still very welcome.

The first landfall rose from the sea. Barbados, palm trees: their first sight of land in weeks. They tied up at the port of Bridgetown. The air was heavy now with a new smell, the sweetness of brown sugar with overtones of rum. The cane sugar was piled mountain-high on the wharf, the layer from each plantation a different colour caused by minerals from the soil, a mountain of sugar in layers of gold, amber, and bronze.

And what was that—a mound of yellow fruit?

A worker flicked his machete and handed Mary the sweetest, most welcome banana she would ever eat.

A small, dirty, square-topsail schooner lay on the other side of the wharf. The troops and their supplies were reloaded onto it, which would transport them on the last leg of the voyage.

William and Mary were at sea again, this time without a cabin, crowded in among cargo and men, their wives, and possessions. They were still five hundred sea miles from Surinam and faced three or four more days of shipboard life without room to lie down.

Barbados slipped away astern as the vessel took a southerly course for Fort Amsterdam, Surinam.

William and Mary felt the oppressive heat of the equator. The whole Guinean Coast seemed an endless dark jungle. Then an opening came in view—the mouth of the Surinam River. The overladen sloop swung its bow toward the river and their first posting. They had no idea what to expect. Their adventures and misadventures were beginning.

Nothing had prepared Mary for the overwhelming sense of isolation of Fort Amsterdam. The fort stood on the equator, surrounded by jungle at the junction of the Commewijne and Surinam Rivers.

The Caribbean sloop sidled up to a makeshift wharf, tied up, and the troops filed ashore. Families followed, all dignity lost, looking filthy, confused, and utterly miserable. Mary, looking on, understood for the first time how relatively privileged she was as an officer's wife. She could appreciate now the full extent of William's responsibility, keep ing order among that rough lot of men when even a card game could turn lethal.

Officers in Surinam during William's time wore uniforms like this. (AUTHOR)

This was not a welcoming place. The first European settlers to move there came by way of Barbados looking for more land on which to grow sugar cane, and thirty thousand slaves were brought from Africa.

Soon the Dutch captured the colony and took over the plantations and their slaves. These slaves rebelled in 1726 and thousands escaped into the jungle and settled inland along the rivers.

Then the British invaded and a treaty awarded this tropical land to the Netherlands in exchange for a cold, hard slice of the Atlantic Coast of North America, which is today New York City. We now know who got the better bargain.

Surinam was the site of a slave rebellion decades before Mary and William arrived. (AUTHOR)

Again, in 1804, William's regiment retook Surinam from the Dutch. William's newly arrived regimental force would replenish the numbers and defend Surinam and its river forts from further attacks. This was the world William and Mary were to live in for the next four years.

A stone building became William and Mary's new home—two small rooms, one for sleeping, and a living room. It was palatial compared to the barracks for the rank and file, nineteen men to one room where they slept, ate, and spent their off-duty hours.

Each man was served one-and-a-half pounds of bread, one pound of potatoes, and three-quarter pound of boiled salt meat. (Half rations for women and quarter rations for children.)

Sometimes the local people (Arawak and Carib tribes) brought "bush meat" to the gates in exchange for tobacco. It could be alligator, anaconda, but in most cases it was Tapir, a pony-sized, five-hundred-pound animal that looks like a pig with a short elephant trunk.

The jungle offered a rich, rotten fragrance that Mary would never forget: a mixture of heady blossoms, of animals, smoke, and privies.

William returned to their quarters from the ramparts one evening after his officer-of-the-watch duties. He was feeling sick, his head and muscles ached, and he was feverish. He had sent half a dozen men back to barracks with the same problems. One of them looked jaundiced. Yellow Jack, perhaps, known today as yellow fever. At that time, no one knew how it spread. The female of one tropical species of mosquito, *aedes aegypti*, carried the virus from one victim to another. Clouds of small zebra-striped mosquitoes (the same species that spreads Zika today) kept the soldiers on the ramparts slapping. Yellow fever has three stages: flu-like symptoms for the first three or four days; a one-day remission period in which many recover; then a period of "intoxication" where heart, liver, and kidneys fail, and the body turns yellow, followed by death.

A capuchin monkey similar to the one that baby William had as a playmate. It was a curious creature with a tail as long as its body. (AUTHOR)

William was better on the fourth day. He would live. Hundreds of his troops did not. Over five hundred British soldiers and twenty-five officers died of Yellow Jack in Surinam. Mary hated mosquitoes. Her insistence on packing mosquito netting had probably saved her.

She befriended one of the bush people who worked at the fort and in the cookhouse. The woman spoke Taki Taki, Sranantongo, the local language, and she would be of great help and comfort to Mary in the next four years.

In 1810, Mary announced she was pregnant again. The baby would be due in December.

William was concerned that without some assistance the delivery would be a lonely ordeal. The cheerful young woman who always helped Mary was obviously delighted as she watched Mary's increasing size. "Doan worry, doan worry. I catch him good." Catch him she did, and baby William was waiting when his delighted father came home from his tour up the river.

As a toddler, baby William's best friend and playmate was a small woolly capuchin monkey, a refugee from the jungle. Known as the "organ grinder's monkey," it weighed only two or three pounds.

Word came in 1812 that their posting was over. They were going home.

They had survived yellow fever and had rejoiced in the birth of William, now a lively two-year-old. Best of all, they would see their daughter, Mary, for the first time in four years. They would sail to Barbados on the *Isabella* and then on to Liverpool on the troopship *Irlam*.

VOYAGE HOME

The ten officers, sixty-two soldiers, thirty-two wives and children boarded the ship for Barbados where the West Indiaman *Irlam* was loading sugar and cotton for England. The 380-ton barque was commanded by Captain George Keyzar, a highly experienced skipper who had sailed the Liverpool to Barbados route for years. In those days, a ship's captain calculated his position at sea using sun or star sightings with his sextant.

Exactly at noon the captain measured the angle of the sun above the horizon with his sextant, read off his position on his "Lat/Long" table, and transferred that position to his chart. The captain would give the order, "Make it noon," and the noon watch would begin. The half-hour sand glass would be turned and thirty minutes later turned again, and a one-bell ring would be struck. "All's well" was called out from each lookout station throughout the ship. This procedure was repeated at each half hour, ending the four-hour watch with eight bells with a change of officer of the watch, helmsmen, and lookouts.

However, ships could sail for days through fog, rain, or storm and never see star or sun. When that happened, the master had to rely on dead reckoning: estimating his position based on the elapsed time since his last known position. Dead reckoning was often dead wrong.

As the *Irlam* made its northward voyage along North America that April, 1812, trouble was brewing between the American Colonies and England, and by July they would be engaged in the War of 1812, setting the future course of William's life and that of his family.

The *Irlam* picked up the Gulf Stream between Cuba and Florida, which carried them up the coast of America to Cape Hatteras, passing south of the Grand Banks. Steady winds, what sailors call the "westerlies," pushed them across the Atlantic to the coast of Ireland. As it got progressively foggier, sextant navigation became impossible.

Three weeks into the voyage they were off the south coast of Ireland, but exactly where was uncertain. They hadn't seen sun nor star for five days.

Somewhere to the north lay Mizen Head, Ireland's most south-westerly point on the treacherous coast.

The *Irlam* moved steadily eastward south of Ireland. Forty-nine days of travel had brought them off the Hook Head lighthouse where the North Atlantic meets the Irish Sea.

Captain Keyzar couldn't spot that light, but he altered course northward toward Liverpool. He had made a fatal error; his dead reckoning position was wrong and his ship was bearing down on a huge outcropping seven miles off Wexford—Tuskar Rock, which had claimed more ships than any other navigational hazard on the Irish coast. It was about to claim one more. There was no warning. At four in the morning the wooden ship slammed into Tuskar Rock with a thundering crash.

William and Mary and their toddler were thrown from their bunk. Their world turned upside down. The cold water rushed into the forecastle and the hold. Troops and their half-dressed families scrambled up to deck and were met with a tangle of smashed life-boats, spars, ropes, cables, and sails. The ship was on her side and starting to break up in the pounding surf.

A lighthouse that might have saved them was under construction on Tuskar Rock. But workmen, who were sleeping there, rescued most of them by throwing ropes over the thirty-nine-foot cliff and hauling up the survivors.

A man, a woman, and three children died, but thankfully, William, Mary, their child, and his monkey survived.

Children were placed in canvas bags and hauled up the cliff. One of these bags held a small toddler, William Junior, and his very wet monkey.

William and Mary lost everything. They were awarded £70 compensation for their loss.

HOME AGAIN

Two weeks later they were home in Cork. The reunion was noisy and tearful.

Mary was getting reacquainted with the daughter they had left in Cork and enjoying the warmth and the loving companionship of family and children. Their third child, Edward Irlam Ross, was born on January 3, 1813, his middle name that of the ship that sank under them. Later that year William's regiment was posted to Ireland, to, of all places, Ross Castle in Killarney, a famous fourteenth-century stronghold that had been converted to military barracks—a palatial setting in a delightful countryside, a sharp contrast to Surinam.

That was not to last. Another foreign posting came in the winter of 1814—to the Canadas, now Quebec and Ontario. The War of 1812 was still raging and there was need of reinforcements. Mary was chagrined—another primitive wilderness posting with ice and snow. Mary would have preferred rain, heat, and hurricanes.

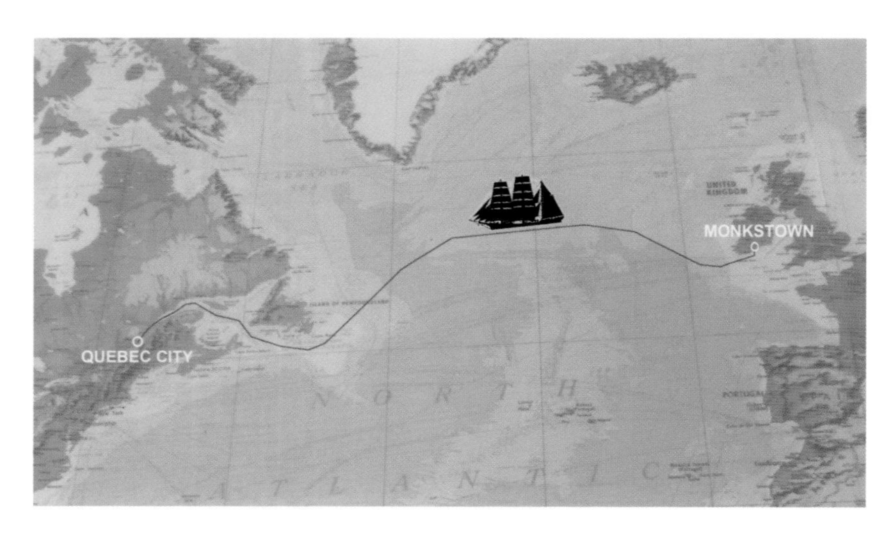

This is the route that the Ross family, which now included three children, took across the Atlantic to the Canadas. They sailed from Ireland to Quebec City. (MURRAY CREED GRAPHIC)

CHAPTER TWO

IN HIS MAJESTY'S SERVICE: THE CANADAS

In the spring of 1814, the family prepared for another Atlantic Ocean voyage, their third in six years, and this time with three small children. They were sailing into war.

The trip would follow the course of the Vikings and Champlain across the North Atlantic. They passed just south of Iceland and Greenland across the Grand Banks where French, Spanish, Portuguese, Nova Scotian, and Newfoundland fishing fleets were handlining for cod.

Thousands of seabirds swirled over the wooden schooners, whose small dories were hauling in huge cod from the seabed one hundred feet below.

After a cold forty-day journey across the Atlantic, the ship sailed up the St. Lawrence River past high, forested hills on the north shore and green farmland on the south, verdant in the summer sun. This was a pleasant surprise to William and Mary. They expected it to be colder and wilder. This looked promising.

QUEBEC CITY

But first a scene from the past: William and his troops formed up on the dock and marched up the hill through fortifications to the barracks in the Quebec City Old Town.

The Ross family was moving into an active war zone. Quebec City was relatively safe with its strong fortifications and a hundred miles of rough forest separating it overland from the advancing Americans. The whole Great Lakes shoreline and the St. Lawrence River from Kingston to Montreal was their target. They had sacked and burned York, now Toronto, and attacked Kingston and Gananoque.

The Ross family boarded a small river sloop for Fort Wellington, situated midway between Fort Henry at Kingston, and Montreal. This crude fort was described "as a clumsy, ill-constructed great mass of earth with a large wooden blockhouse." It was hardly a welcoming site.

This was William and Mary's seventh posting since marriage. Schooling the children was up to Mary. She did her best to teach her eight-year-old daughter basic math and English.

In September, the regiment was moved again, to Fort Coteau du Lac just outside Montreal to reinforce a Nova Scotia Fencibles Regiment, which had done garrison duty there since the beginning of the war. This fort was built to prevent the Americans from storming up from Lake Champlain and capturing Montreal. It would be home for the Ross family for the remainder of their stay in the Canadas.

A stone building was divided into six rooms, each with twelve bunks, to accommodate 288 soldiers who slept on straw mattresses that stank and crawled with lice known as a "donkey's breakfast"—although no self-respecting donkey would go near them. In winter, fuel was scarce so it was cold, damp, and dark. The officers' quarters were not much better.

The Treaty of Ghent ended the war the day before Christmas 1814. Fate stepped in again for William and his family. William had met Lieutenant Edward Davidson of the Nova Scotia regiment, whose family had immigrated to Nova Scotia from Ireland when he was eleven. He had joined the Nova Scotia Fencibles and been posted to Coteau du Lac at the beginning of the war. He was full of tales of Nova Scotia.

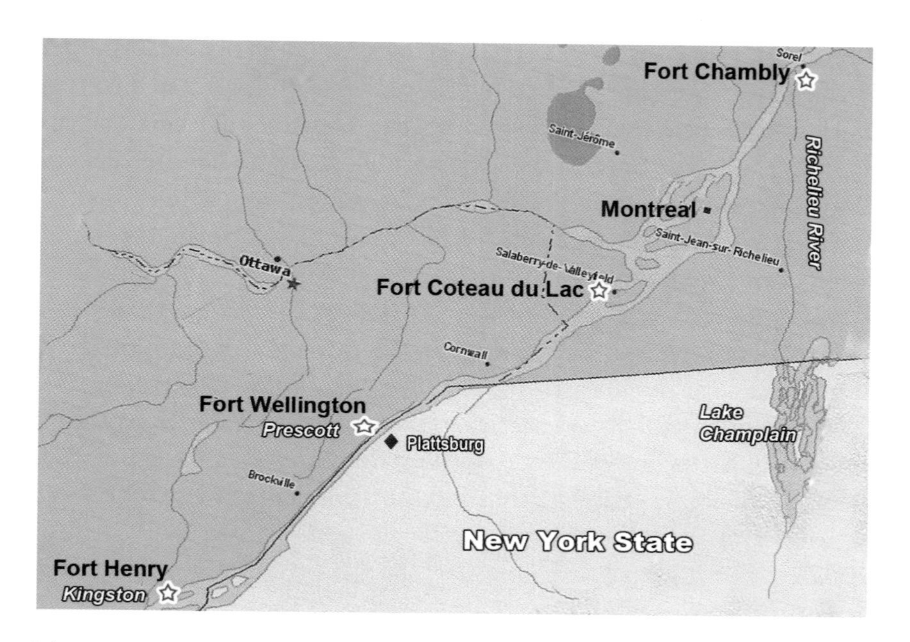

There were many fortifactions to defend the area of Fort Wellington where the Ross family was living during this troubled time. (MURRAY CREED GRAPHIC)

When the Fencibles regiments were formed, recruiting posters drew in volunteers with promises of free rich and fertile land and every luxury of life at war's end. The "free" part came true but not the "rich and fertile" nor the "every luxury of life" parts of the offer.

Orders came down that 16th Regiment of Foot would be shipped back to Britain and that the Nova Scotia Fencibles would be disbanded and offered land grants. By this time, William and his new friend, Davidson, had a plan. Davidson wanted to get back to Ireland. William wanted a new challenge, and coming from Ireland where landowners were wealthy and revered, the idea of free land in Nova Scotia was irresistible. If William and Edward could switch regiments, they could both realize their dreams. Their transfers were approved.

William's new commanding officer, Lieutenant Colonel Darling of the Fencibles had been watching William perform his duties. He saw him as mature and trustworthy, just the kind of man he had in mind to lead an operation he had been ordered to undertake—the settlement of a tract of land along an unfinished military road into the interior of Nova Scotia. Darling had found his man—William.

In September 1815, another son was born to William and Mary—George, the baby who would carry the Ross bloodline and heritage to this day in Nova Scotia. His siblings, Mary, eleven, William, five, and Edward, three, took turns rocking the baby.

William, who was by now on the strength of the Nova Scotia Fencibles, sailed for Halifax in the spring of the following year—1816.

ANOTHER SHIPWRECK

In the last week of May 1816, William, Mary, and their four children set sail from Quebec City for Halifax on the Royal Navy troopship H.M.S. *Archduke Charles,* commanded by an experienced master, Captain P. H. Brown.

As the eight hundred rank and file, twelve officers, forty-seven women and children filed aboard, the mood was optimistic. William and Mary were going to their new home—Nova Scotia.

When they cleared the St. Lawrence River and Gulf, Captain Brown set a course along the coast of Nova Scotia that would bring them just off Halifax. Fog made sun or star sightings impossible and Captain Brown's dead reckoning positioning was adrift. He altered course too soon on the night of June 28, 1816, bringing the ship too close to shore.

Without warning, a thunderous impact of ship and rock slammed people from their bunks, tangled together below deck in the darkness. Seawater rushed in; men, women, and children were

An old drawing of the Gulf Stream featuring Nova Scotia, which became the Ross family's final home. (AUTHOR)

up to their waists in ice-cold water. The wooden hull was ruptured, half of the starboard side ripped away by the jagged rock face as it rose and fell repeatedly with each breaking sea.

William, Mary, and the children struggled onto deck. When he got them safely huddled in the lee of a deckhouse, William tried without too much success to bring order out of chaos among his troops. It became a sad example of "every man for himself."

This dramatic shipwreck story appeared in newspapers around the world and as far away as New Zealand:

> The *Archduke Charles*, transport, Captain Brown left Quebec on May 29, 1816 with the Right Wing of the Royal Nova Scotia Fencibles, under Colonel Darling. There were on board, in addition to the crew, 11 officers, over 800 rank and file, and 48 women and children.

> At about 7 in the evening she was gradually begirt by the infamous black ring, which showed she was within the grasp of the fogbank. There was no means of escape, and so, as she was in the "track of the homeward-bound" West India ships, she was put under easy sail, and precautions were taken against collision. Look-outs were stationed fore and aft peering out into the night, and the drummers were ordered on deck to keep their drums going as a caution to all that passed. Drum, drum, drum, drum, and drum.

The vessel settled into the seas, her decks awash, and men climbed into her rigging, thick as bees. Up in the bow, one of William's fellow officers, Lieutenant Charles Stewart, fastened a half-inch rope around his waist and jumped overboard. He was sucked under the bow but managed to swim to a rock and scrambled up the slippery seaweed and secured his rope. Then the crew rigged a breeches buoy and the troops and their families were taken off the ship one by one. Soon afterwards, the ship broke up.

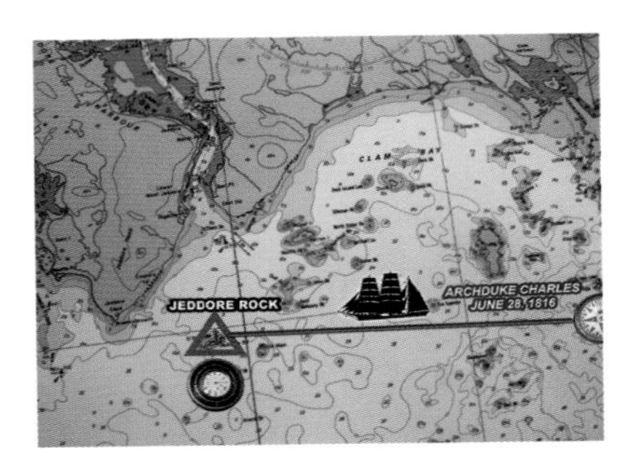

Fishermen from Jeddore, on the Eastern Shore of Nova Scotia, helped rescue shipwreck survivors. (MURRAY CREED GRAPHIC)

HALIFAX AT LAST

Fishermen from Jeddore, Nova Scotia, rowed passengers ashore, wet and shivering. William, Mary, and their four children were taken in and warmed and dried by a kitchen stove, their first taste of Nova Scotia hospitality and kindness. They slept in dry beds and woke up to oatmeal porridge, bread and molasses, tea, and a fresh glass of cold milk for the children.

At noon they walked down to the village wharf, boarded a coastal schooner, and cast off for Halifax. As their ship approached the southern promontory of Halifax Peninsula with it batteries and lookout towers, it veered to the northwest, entered what is now known as the Northwest Arm, and anchored off Melville Island. They were rowed ashore and shown their quarters in an abandoned prison that had held American captives during the war.

Next morning the soldiers, officers, and men walked the three miles to the army barracks by Citadel Hill in Halifax to report for duty and to be discharged. They walked to the head of the Arm, crossed a bridge, and headed up Chebucto Road past the south blockhouse, which guarded the Northwest Arm. They crossed the Commons where cattle and sheep were grazing, past the governor's racetrack and his mansion on the northwest slope of Citadel Hill, and around the fortifications to Barrack Street and army headquarters. William glanced up at the town clock that Prince Edward had built thirteen years earlier and noted that it was almost noon. Further down toward the harbour he saw sixty-five-year-old St. Paul's Church and Province House, which was still under construction. And south in the distance was Government House, new in 1805, all fine buildings that reminded him of home in Cork.

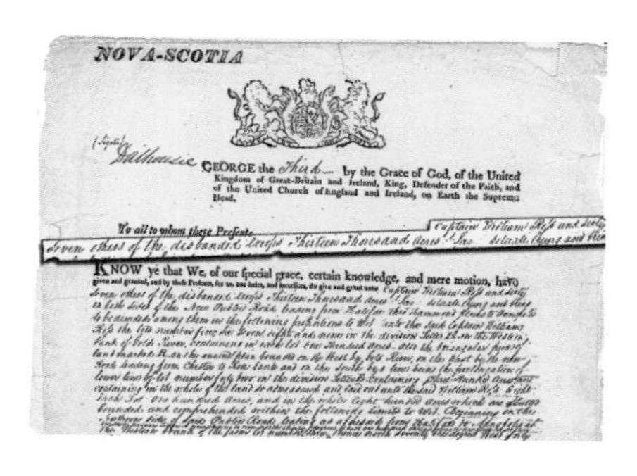
NOVA-SCOTIA

GEORGE the Third by the Grace of God, of the United Kingdom of Great-Britain and Ireland, King, Defender of the Faith, and of the United Church of England and Ireland, on Earth the Supreme Head,

To all to whom these Presents

KNOW ye that We, of our special grace, certain knowledge, and mere motion, have

William received a land grant for a remote area of Nova Scotia then called Sherbrooke. He went ahead of his family to build a home. (AUTHOR)

He reported to his CO, Lieutenant Colonel Darling. William had been chosen to lead 172 ex-Fencibles to a place called Sherbrooke on the Military Road in the interior of the province. He would be made the equivalent of captain but continue on half-pay, as lieutenant. He would be granted eight hundred acres of farmland, which he and his descendants would own in perpetuity. He would also be named magistrate to ensure authority over the disbanded soldiers.

William walked back to Melville Island with a spring in his step. All that land, a promotion to captain, appointed magistrate—he couldn't lose. Mary had concerns. How would they get to the new settlement? There would be no house, no school, no church, and no store. Winter was coming with no time to plant anything. What would they eat? These questions were on William's mind, too.

Rations will be provided, he told her. The government would supply tools. It would be hard but they'd manage. He would go in first and build a log cabin, and come back in the fall to get his family. William would do everything possible to make Mary happy in the new settlement. And he'd have his farm. He'd be a landowner.

Next day William stepped smartly into Darling's office and told him he would accept the undertaking. Darling's military bearing eased, he stepped forward and shook the thirty-three-year-old lieutenant's hand, and said: "Congratulations, *Captain* Ross. You'll have my full support." Then he asked how conditions were where they were quartered on Melville Island. "Grim, Sir," William replied. "We'll get your family out of there soon," said Darling. "I'll introduce you to an old friend, John Lawson, who will take your wife and the children into his home, while you're out there building a cabin for them." That offer was to make Mary's life bearable in the next three months and build friendships that would endure for a lifetime.

William and his 172 pioneering ex-soldiers gathered on King's Wharf in Halifax on August, 1, 1816, boarded the government vessel *Earl of Bathurst,* and set sail for Chester. Mary and the children saw him off and watched until the sail slipped over the horizon past Auger's Beach.

CHAPTER THREE

SETTLING THE ROCKY SPINE OF NOVA SCOTIA

THE SHIP SAILED INTO CHESTER and the men off-loaded tents, axes, and supplies onto the wharf. William was in charge but no longer in uniform. The men still wore remnants of theirs.

William had a hand-drawn map. Their destination, Sherbrooke, was on the map. But there didn't seem to be a road to it. However, another settlement, Sherwood, was halfway along a road from Chester to Windsor. They would walk that road as far as Sherwood, and then find their way through the woods to Sherbrooke.

William and his men hoisted packs, grabbed rifles and axes, and trudged up through the village to the road. They set out with jokes and jibes. Soon sweat poured down their faces, attracting swarms of mosquitoes. There was little to joke about now.

Scratched and bruised after the sixteen-mile trudge, they straggled into Sherwood at sunset. Sherwood had been settled by ex-solders like them, Newfoundland Fencibles, disbanded a year earlier. William's weary men caught a glimpse of what they were to experience: rough log huts and outbuildings, patches of cleared land, one or two cows grazing in the meadow by the lake. Captain Evans, the man in charge at Sherwood, welcomed Ross and his band. He described the twelve miles of bogs, barrens, and streams they would still have to cross to get to their settlement area.

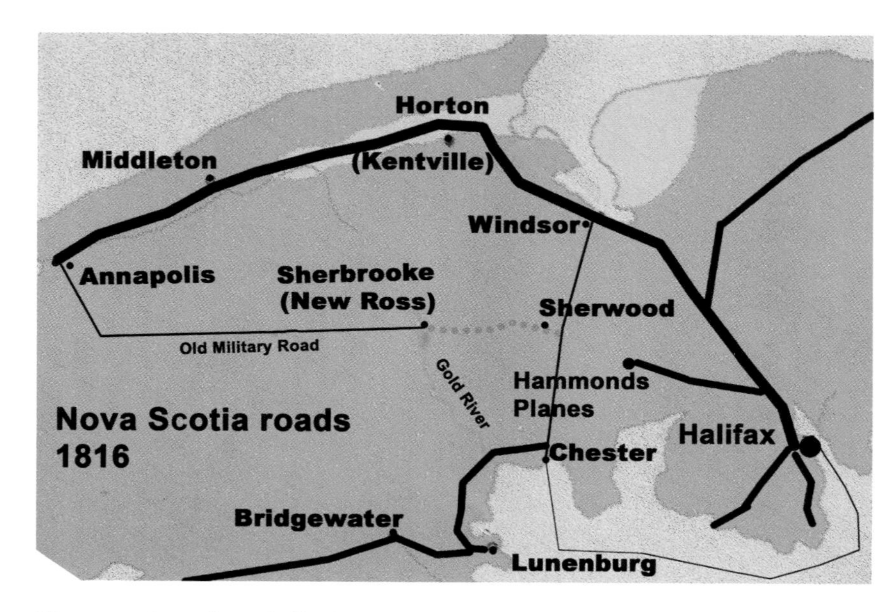

This map shows how difficult it was to reach Sherbrooke in 1816. There was no road from Halifax to the south shore, so the only access was by sailing ship. There was a rutty road from Chester to Windsor. The Old Military Road ran from Annapolis to Sherbrooke, now New Ross. (MURRAY CREED GRAPHIC)

William's men pitched tents, slept briefly, and at dawn, set off again into the wilderness. The mosquitoes were fierce and William wondered if he would have been better off back in the jungles of Surinam. The complaining never stopped.

At sunset they climbed the last hill and saw a deep, still lake and a free-flowing river. William paused and drew a deep breath. Then he saw wild roses; he looked at the hillside and named it Rosebank for Mary. She would get her cottage, but not this year. In the meantime, he would build a log cabin. Soon tents dotted the meadow and campfires blazed. One man threw a fishing line into the lake and caught a ten-pound salmon, which soon sizzled on the fire. They got out hardtack biscuits, lit pipes, and settled in for the night. Tomorrow they would be allocated individual plots of land. The really hard work would now begin.

William was content. As he lay in his bedroll on the hard ground, he thought of Mary in Halifax. Exhausted, he slept. He had become a landowner—one of the first in what was later to be called New Ross.

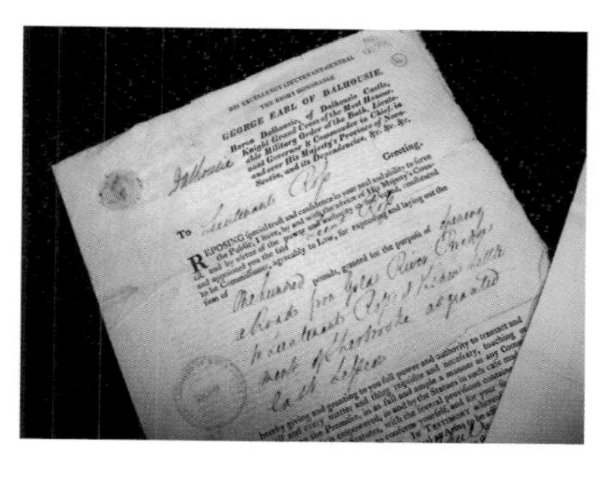
GEORGE EARL OF DALHOUSIE,
Baron Dalhousie, of Dalhousie Castle,
Knight Grand Cross of the Most Honour-
able Military Order of the Bath, Lieutenant Governor & Commander in Chief in
and over His Majesty's Province of Nova-
Scotia, and its Dependencies, &c. &c. &c.
Greeting.
To
REPOSING special trust and confidence in your zeal and ability to serve the Public, I have, by and with the advice of His Majesty's Council, and by virtue of the power and authority to me
and appointed you the said
to be Commissioner, agreeably to Law, for expending and laying out the
sum of
pounds, granted for the purpose of
hereby giving and granting to you full power and authority to transact and
all and every matter and thing requisite and necessary, touching
the Premises, in as full and ample a manner as any Com
empowered, in and by the Statutes in such case
Statutes, with the several provisions contain
conform yourself, and for your
IN TESTIMONY whereof

Some of the land grants were better than others, and some of the early settlers eventually gave up their dream of a new home. This document is signed by The Right Honorable George Earl of Dalhousie. (NOVA SCOTIA ARCHIVES)

FIRST TASKS

On the morning following, a quick breakfast over, the excitement began. Before leaving Halifax, each man had drawn lots for a "Ticket of Location"—their allocated land. Maps and charts were laid out. One-by-one, the men filed by with their numbered tickets and drew for one-hundred-acre plots on William's chart, some of them a mile or more away. Each man then went out to find the matching number on stakes marking the boundary of his assigned hundred acres.

Some of these plots had good potential; some were less desirable. At this point, it all became very real. Some would spend the rest of their lives on the land allotted to them; many homesteads are still owned by their descendants. Others would be defeated by their own lack of practical skills and the hardships they had to endure, and half of them would give up and leave for an easier life in Halifax. Within three years only 68 of the 172 settlers remained.

In the lot plan of land grants, William was awarded five one-hundred-acre lots on Lake Lawson and another two on the lower river, plus a mill lot on the upper Gold River. His friend James Wells received one hundred acres at the upper end of the lake.

William named the lake for John Lawson, the man who gave the Ross family shelter in Halifax. William named a smaller one Lake Darling, honouring his old CO, Lieutenant Colonel Darling.

That first evening William walked over his land and decided where he would build. He chose a spot by Lake Lawson for a temporary log cabin.

From the beginning, rations were provided: biscuits, flour, salt pork, and salt beef, plus a ration of rum, brought in by the puncheon. The rum was probably opened first. The settlers were expected to get the rest of their food from the land, the forest, and the rivers and lakes. But it was too late in the year to plant a crop, so the record-cold winter of 1816 would be a long and hungry one.

Most of these men, including William, had no knowledge of farming, carpentry, or lumbering. Trees had to be felled, trimmed up, and cut into logs. "Burning frolics" came next, in which neighbours gathered to roll the logs into piles and burned them. These giant bonfires lasted for days. Tree stumps were left to rot for at least a year before an attempt was made to remove them. At first this was all done by manpower. Later that fall, oxen were brought in from Lunenburg to haul logs and help pull the stumps. Ox teams became the main source of power and are still used on Ross Farm today.

In *History of New Ross,* Caroline Leopold writes: "Captain William Ross cut down the first tree, probably the first ever felled by him. It was a rock maple from which a dining table and a dozen egg-cups were later made. The table is still preserved at New Ross."

Above the slope from Lake Lawson, William marked a flat area where he would eventually build his cottage.

Author J. Lynton Martin in *The Ross Farm Story* writes about pioneering days in the community, land clearing, and farming methods, and illustrates the tools and implements they used, many designed and made from wood, iron, and ingenuity. He writes: "Nova Scotia is divided into two geological types: the Lowlands, such as the Annapolis Valley which constitute our best agricultural lands, and the Uplands which make up most of the province, which feature rough forested, rocky lands with small disconnected patches of tillable soil, averaging 20 acres in size."

William tackled one of those twenty-acre patches of land on Ross Farm. He picked up his English felling axe, and with the help of a neighbour piled the brush and set it on fire. The larger spruce and pine were used to build cabins, the hardwood cut and split for firewood, and the tall straight poles set aside for fencing. The rest they left to dry for burning next spring when the neighbours gathered for a burning frolic. The ashes provided natural fertilizer for the potatoes they would hoe in between the tree roots.

After William had built a log cabin, Mary and the children were able to join him. Pictured is a Ross Farm Museum staff member dressed as Mary may have looked at the time. (ROSS FARM)

And when he had built a rough log cabin shelter for his family, he returned to Halifax for Mary and the children. He wrapped his arms around Mary, and when he could compose himself, William said, "Your home is waiting."

William and Mary with their four children, ages ten, six, three, and one, boarded the coastal vessel next morning for Chester, one of the most meaningful steps in the Ross family saga.

In all likelihood, William hired a horse and cart to take them up the Windsor Road to Sherwood where they would have stayed overnight with Captain Evans and his family. From there they probably walked the twelve-mile route William had taken through the woods to Rosebank. The two older children would have walked—very slowly—but the three-year-old and the baby probably had to be carried. Exhausted, each mile they trudged seemed twice as long as the last one.

Finally, they came to the hill where William had stood, looking over his land for the first time, and there in the distance was a small log cabin.

"Ours?" Mary asked.

"Ours," replied William.

William opened the door and proudly led his family into the log cabin. Mary saw her kitchen with a fireplace, a table and chairs, all of which she knew William had made. And in the second room he'd built bunk beds on one wall for the boys, a narrow bed on the opposite wall for their daughter, and a double bed against a third wall for them.

Mary, the stoic that she was, accepted the rough cabin, knowing that all she had endured and accepted came down to this—a cabin at the end of a rough road, deep in the wilderness. At last, after eleven years of marriage, they owned a home and her children were safe from the sea.

She looked out across the shining lake. It was the view that would be a constant comfort in her life—come what may.

THEIR FIRST LIVESTOCK

A letter arrived from Halifax, bearing welcome news: the gift of a cow to be brought from Lunenburg to Chester, where William must pick it up.

It was late fall when a very tired William led the lanky, limping, brown-spotted cow along the path through the woods out to the

Little by little, the Ross family farm began to acquire livestock such as these steers that are now part of the museum. (MATTHEW GATES)

clearing at Rosebank Cottage where Mary was waiting with the children. "Bring her some water," he said, and his daughter lugged a wooden pail full of lake water to the cow. She emptied the pail without stopping.

In *The Ross Farm Story*, J. Lynton Martin describes the cow as:

> The most valuable animal on the pioneer farm by far. She provided milk, butter and cheese for the family, skim milk and buttermilk for the pigs and chickens. Male offspring were trained to work under the yoke and provide the chief source of farm power until just before 1900. She provided beef for the table and leather for footwear and harness, and her manure was put back on the land to enrich the soil.

Farm families named their milk cows, as they would be around for years and were milked twice a day, making them almost part of

Milk was kept cool in a hollowed-out log in a spring under the trees by the lake. The cream rose to the top. The heavier skim milk was drawn out through a plugged spigot in the bottom of the log. Later a stone crock replaced the log.

The first butter churn was a homemade wooden tub with a hole in the cover. A cross-shaped plunger on the end of a straight wooden rod worked it up and down through the hole, churning the cream. It took hours of work to produce butter. Women and children of the household took turns. The fresh butter was removed and salted to preserve it and improve the taste. The leftover buttermilk went to the pigs and chickens, some of it kept aside for baking.

Butter churns were important devices for early farmers. (AUTHOR)

J. Lynton Martin writes:

> The amount of labour involved in churning butter is indicated by the fact that after 1835 many new churn designs were patented in Nova Scotia, all seeking to reduce the hard work and the time involved. Some preferred box churns on wooden rockers so that granny could continue to knit or mend or tend the baby while her foot rocked the churn.
>
> As time passed, family farms favoured the small rotary churn, and larger farms turned to the barrel churn on a metal frame. DeLaval invented the cream separator in 1878, greatly simplifying butter making.

the family. Beef cattle were generally not named—too hard to kill them if they had a name. It was the same with pigs and poultry. Horses were given names but not oxen. Curiously, an ox team was always called Bright and Lion—Bright on the right and Lion on the left. William had built a small barn to house the cow, a couple of pigs, and some poultry.

In the winter of 1818, worry crept into the home along with snow that blew under the doorstep. Both brought a chill that lingered all winter and into spring. A modest amount of help came from an unexpected place. One morning Mary looked up to see a dark face peering in the window. Her visitor was a Mi'kmaq. He was holding out a frozen slab of meat—moose, it turned out. When Mary got up the courage to open the door he was gone—the meat lay on the snow at her feet. It was the beginning of a friendship.

NEIGHBOURS

In Cork, where William and Mary grew up, neighbours were just people who lived next door, most little more than nodding acquaintances. Family was close.

In primitive 1816 Sherbrooke (New Ross), the reverse was true. Family was distant, thousands of miles across the Atlantic, and neighbours meant everything: company in a lonely land and help with the many things one person couldn't manage alone, from sawing a log with a pit saw, raising a rafter, to birthing a baby. Together, neighbours rolled and burned trash logs, raised barns, and threshed grain. A few brought special skills: blacksmithing, midwifery, and teaching.

William and Mary's neighbour across the lake became the first teacher for Sherbrooke. James Wells was a twenty-seven-year-old Oxford-educated ex-Royal Navy officer who had been enticed to join the settlement for that specific job. He and his wife were granted one hundred acres on the north end of Lake Lawson, and their house was visible from William and Mary's. To visit, they walked around the lake in summer and across the ice in winter.

On one of these visits Wells brought out two sets of navy semaphore flags, a convenient way to communicate. William took one pair of flags home, got out his old code book, and practised. Next day he went down by the lake and sent his first message—R-O-S-S.

Slowly life at the new settlement improved socially and spiritually. The first church service took place in the Ross home in 1817. Reverend Charles Inglis from Chester preached a sermon based on Isaiah 2: 4, *"And they shall beat their swords into ploughshares."* William could be excused if he chuckled. We don't know if he still had his sword, probably not, but we do know that he didn't have a plow and wouldn't have one for several years, as the authorities in Halifax considered he did not have enough land cleared to justify receiving one.

In 1818, £100 was allocated to build a school. The first church was built in 1824, Christ Church Anglican, served by a minister from Chester. St. Patrick Roman Catholic Church opened in 1827 and a Baptist church in 1831.

William Kearney, the first medical doctor, arrived in 1835, nineteen years after the settlers had arrived at Sherbrooke. Home remedies and some highly valued tonics shipped from relatives were all they had. The Mi'kmaq helped the locals identify herbal remedies.

Social life thrived as neighbours gathered for frolics—burning frolics; mowing frolics to cut the meadow with scythes; building frolics to erect houses, barns, and outbuildings; quilting and rug-hooking frolics where the women gathered to make quilts to cover beds and mats to cover drafty floors. When the work was done, the frolicking began.

Neighbours dropped in without invitation, shared a cup of tea or a drink of rum punch, and stayed overnight if the weather got nasty, curling up anywhere they could find a spot to lie down, often near the kitchen stove. A plaid-covered cot in the kitchen was a necessity. The man of the house could flop there in his grubby work clothes before returning in the afternoon to work. The main

The Ross family and their neighbours often congregated after the daily chores were done. Those chores included taking care of livestock like the pigs now on the farm. (MATTHEW GATES)

meal, dinner, was served at noon, followed by a nap. Work continued until sundown. The evening meal, supper, was served at five o'clock. The men went back out to work in the fields until dark, while the women fed the animals and milked the cows, supervised the kids' chores, and cleaned up dishes and laundry.

Mi'kmaw people dropped by. They would appear at the door with a salmon or a quarter of deer meat and be welcomed in for a visit and a mug-up. In contrast to the brutality of early Halifax and Governor Cornwallis's bounty on the head of every Mi'kmaq, these early settlers realized that in New Ross at least, Indigenous people were their friends and teachers in practical matters of how to survive in this demanding land.

It soon became evident that a promised road eastward from Sherbrooke through Sherwood to Hammonds Plains would never be built. Instead, a more practical trail southward toward Chester Basin would be opened (Route 12, today).

In *History of New Ross*, Caroline Leopold recounts a tragedy that illustrates the condition of the road in its early years: "Some men going through Seffern's Swamp one day saw a man's hat floatin' around on top of the mud. Pokin' around with poles, they found, buried in the mud, the body of a man, two horses, and a wagonload of oat straw."

Twenty years later, William and Mary's son, Edward, noted in his diary that Sherbrooke to Chester Basin could be travelled in a day, and it was over this route that Edward hauled his produce for sale in Halifax and returned with Halifax-bought goods for sale in his Sherbrooke store.

Slowly but surely, Sherbrooke became connected with the rest of Nova Scotia, but for at least another generation, the settlers would have to rely on their neighbours for most of their daily needs and for their social life.

When William built his permanent home in 1817, there was still no sawmill in Sherbrooke. That great labour-saving device would not be available until the next year, so William was forced

The Ross family and settlers like them became more and more proficient in farming. The traditional methods are preserved today. (MATTHEW GATES)

to cut and square his timbers with a broad axe and an adze and, with the help of a neighbour, saw his boards with a pit saw.

Here's how Caroline Leopold describes it in her *History of New Ross:*

> The boards were sawed by two men, one standing above the log on a frame on which the log was laid, the other in a "saw pit" below the log. With each up and down pull, the saw bit into the log lengthways, ripping out a one-inch board and showering the man in the pit with wet sawdust, sticky with pine or spruce sap. The first boards were anything but even, perhaps one inch at one end and two at the other, with wobbles in between. But after a few cuts they learned to control the saw better and the cuts were straighter. The uneven boards were used where they wouldn't show.

J. Lynton Martin writes in *The Ross Farm Story:*

Rosebank Cottage was different from the usual timber frame dwelling, but typical of many homes built in Lunenburg County. Rather than being boarded in the usual manner, the corner posts were grooved, and solid plank walls, three to four inches thick, were built up with the ends of the planks reduced to fit the grooves in the posts. Split hemlock lath was placed in the inside walls and ceilings and they were then plastered.

It was solid construction indeed, construction that lasts to this day, two centuries later. Visitors to Ross Farm Museum can stand in Mary's place at the hearth, look at the walls that William built, and get a sense of their lives. A visitor is often invited to have tea and a hot biscuit from a pioneer recipe. Martin continues:

> The cottage was built around a central flue with five fireplaces. The one in the cellar was lighted in winter during very cold nights to prevent potatoes and vegetables from freezing. The kitchen fireplace had a built-in oven to provide all cooking needs. The three other hearths, one in the dining room, one in the parlour and one upstairs served to heat the house.

It was no small feat to build such a chimney with five working fireplaces from field rocks gathered on the property. These fireplaces, including the built-in oven, are still used today.

Meanwhile the Ross family was increasing. They needed room for four small children, plus a baby, due any day. William was building a home for Mary that remains on Ross Farm Museum—Rosebank Cottage.

FIRST CROPS

William had eaten his share of potatoes in Ireland, although he had never grown a single one. His fellow countrymen relied on spuds as the main staple in their diets, more important than bread. Even in those days before the Irish potato famine, people almost starved when potato crops failed

Caroline Leopold writes: "In 1817, Captain Ross received among other things, seed potatoes (five bushels for each actual settler), turnip seed, red and white clover seed, shovels, garden rakes, Dutch bake ovens, fishing nets, rope, lead, cork and even trout hooks, twine, wax and thread."

The settlers were now equipped to plant their first crops, and to try for trout and salmon in the lake at their doorstep.

Even though he was born in Ireland, William was a city boy and did not grow his first potato until he started his own farm in Nova Scotia. (ROSS FARM)

Preparing the soil for potatoes was not as much fun as fishing. William had cleared small areas of the smaller trees, "grubbed out" roots with a German claw hoe, and burned off the brush, loosened the blackened soil with his burnt-land hoe, and carefully planted pieces of potato. In two days, he was finished. When the plants developed, he would pick off potato bugs and hope that blight or frost wouldn't kill the plants before harvest time.

He planted the clover seed broadcast style, stepping slowly, spreading the tiny seeds with a sweep of his arm, and raking a light layer of soil over the seed. The tiny turnip seed was planted in shallow rows and gently covered. When the plants came up, he would thin them with his hoe, leaving a plant every six inches.

His spring planting was finally done; every inch of cleared ground had been put to use. Next year he would have a lot more cleared land, perhaps a whole field, enough for a respectable farm crop.

Now that they had Patches the cow, William needed to put up a winter's supply of hay. Nova Scotia is famous for its abundant grass production, almost as good as back home in Ireland. The meadow down by the lake was lush and green, and he set out to turn it into hay. The government didn't provide implements for harvesting hay and grain—no one thought that far ahead. William needed a scythe, a rake, and a fork. He could make the rake and the fork himself, but in a community without a forge he would have to buy the scythe blade in Halifax. The wooden handle, he made from a slender hardwood tree.

He took his new harvesting tool down to the meadow where no one could see, and practised. On his first try, the tip of the scythe blade started low and swung high, cutting off just the heads of the timothy and clover. On the second swing, the tip dug into the ground. On the third try, he got it right, always keeping the blade parallel to the ground. He soon mastered the sweep, and saw the freshly cut grass lying in a neat swath behind him. Those moments of gratification were so welcome.

He found a small sapling with three almost parallel branches. This became his fork. Then he made a rake with pegs for teeth. He built small wooden pyramids on which he laid the grass to dry. Now that he had the tools, he called the older children to help. He cut the grass, and they raked and coiled it on the drying pyramids. Two days later, the hay was ready to stack. He criss-crossed slim rails for the base to keep the hay off the ground and prevent rotting. Then he and the children forked layer after layer of the newly sun-cured hay on the platform. He cut a ten-foot square of tent canvas, laid it over the top, and weighted it down with rocks tied to the corners. Patches now had her winter's feed. It was late summer, and soon it would be time to harvest the grain.

J. Lynton Martin writes:

> The pioneer's grain was scattered by hand on the burnt land and covered with soil with the burnt-land harrow—and on particularly

rough land with the hoe. When ripe, the grain was harvested with the sickle or reaping hook. The women often helped with this task, either reaping or tying up the sheaves. It was slow, hard work and required 15 to 20 hours for one person to reap an acre.

He adds: "One of the first thoughts of the pioneer farmer was to raise enough wheat for his bread. Imported flour was expensive and money to purchase it was scarce. But weather conditions often prevented ripening and the flour ground from it was of poor quality."

Next came the thrashing. William fashioned a flail from a maple sapling. He then cut an eight-inch strip of eel skin and tied the two pieces together. The result was a flail. He spread another piece of tent canvas on the ground where he placed a sheaf of grain. He whacked grain off the straw with every swing of his homemade flail. He shovelled the grain and chaff into a homemade winnowing basket, shook it, and most of the light chaff blew away, leaving the grains behind ready for grinding.

THE MOOSE HUNT

Edward and George, and Dick and Frank Russell, men who lived in the area, went on a moose hunt one spring morning before sunrise. Moose meat was highly prized for its mild flavour and tenderness. Everything from the tongue to the tail—and the valuable hide—was used up. In fact the nose, called the muffle, was a delicacy and considered the prime cut.

British chef Fergus Henderson has recently published two cookbooks: *The Whole Beast– Nose to Tail Eating* and its sequel, *Beyond Nose and Tail*. He writes: "A moose muffle is the nose and the pendulous, overhanging upper lip of the moose which was eaten by the Cree as a delicacy; boiled, baked, or fried." For the hunter to give a friend a muffle was considered a high compliment. But when Edward was given one by a Mi'kmaq, he gave grudging thanks to the donor.

While Edward was usually put off by the cooking habits of the area's Indigenous people, he was quick enough to adopt their innovations. They made cooking pots of wood or birchbark, and superheated rocks were taken from the coals and gradually added to water in the frail pots until the water boiled and their food cooked.

Clothes were hung out to dry like this at the farm in the days before modern conveniences. (MATTHEW GATES)

HOUSEWORK AT ROSEBANK

The first Rosebank Cottage had no conveniences to help Mary with cooking and cleaning. Often times pregnant, she scrubbed floors with vinegar, carried pails filled with slops, lugged water from the lake, and carried wood for the fire.

It would be 1907 before the first flush toilet, so privies provided the only comfort.

Although Mary would die in 1876, so she did see that marvel of convenience the washing machine, equipped with a wringer, the power for which was produced by the woman of the household. The handle was cranked according to precise directions. Adjustable rollers, also activated by a crank and gearing system, would not only wring out the last drop of water from the clothes, but leave the operator wrung out as well.

GOVERNOR ON HORSEBACK

George Ramsay, 9th Earl of Dalhousie, a Scottish landed nobleman known in Britain as "Farmer George," arrived in Nova Scotia as governor in October 1816. Wounded in a Napoleonic War battle, he walked with a limp but was still an excellent horseman and travelled widely during his four years as governor of Nova Scotia.

One of his journeys was to visit the Sherbrooke farming settlement. Lieutenant Colonel Darling, his military secretary, wrote to William on March 4, 1817, "The Governor intends to visit the settlement probably in May. His lordship is planning, to come fish trout and salmon before the flies bite."

He probably was a little late—the blackflies would be out in full force by then. William was also instructed to "clear as much land as possible before Lord Dalhousie's visit to the settlement"—as if he had nothing else to do.

In August 1818, well after blackfly season, Governor Dalhousie sailed from Halifax to Chester, hired "two country ponies," and he and his aide-de-camp rode in to Sherbrooke settlement. His diary entrees tell the story:

> Lt. Ross of the Nova Scotia Fencibles, of which 100 of the men settled here are the remains, came to meet us. Mr. Ross, an Irishman, resolved on sharing their hardships and had done a great deal in the way of example, and by encouragement, but for want of a system on the part of the Government when first placing them here, they have had to contend with the most appalling difficulties.
>
> The road to Ross' hut is scarcely passible, what with rock, bogs and rotten logs I never could have hoped to accomplish the end without broken legs and arms.
>
> However we did reach his place, which he calls Rosebank in about four and a half hours. He had prepared a very good dinner for us and invited his neighbour, Mr. Wells, an officer of the navy, whose distressing circumstances have let him to fix there as a schoolmaster for the sake of getting land and rations.
>
> Mrs. Wells, a remarkably pretty woman, and very ladylike…she

had been obliged to go out there in May, the snow so deep even then that she got into a wretched log house and during the first month kept warm by the thickness of the smoke.

Mrs. Ross is also lively and pleasant, but more able and more used to hardship. Her eldest girl is able to help a little. She also appears happy and contented.

Several of the settlers do their work industriously and have cleared large pieces of land—10-15 acres and will do well. But two-thirds of their number will leave the settlement as soon as rations cease.

I shall, as soon as I return to Halifax, send down a detachment of regiment to make a road accessible to Halifax.

A letter arrived March 19, 1817, informing William that "The legislature has voted 600 pounds toward opening and improving that road from Sherbrooke to Hammond's Plains." But the money did little toward building the cross-country route laid out for the Old Military Road from Annapolis to Halifax via Hammonds Plains. The road lay untouched until four years later. In 1822, it was to play a fateful role in the lives of William and Mary Ross. The governor did send soldiers, not a whole detachment, but only four of them. They came not to build a road but to bring a present.

THE PIANO THAT KILLED RABBITS

Four soldiers stumbled, sweating, out of the woods and set their heavy burden down on the grass in front of Rosebank Cottage. They had carried it all the way from Chester Basin. The box contained a Broadwood piano for twelve-year-old Mary Ross, a gift from Governor Dalhousie.

William ran his callused hand over the polished wood and thought to himself, "Better he had sent us a plow."

When Mary married Andrew Kiens in 1827, the piano was moved to their home across Lake Lawson. Edward, her brother, made several diary entries such as: "went to Mary's to hear the piano." When she died in 1850 the piano was returned to Rosebank Cottage. It was small comfort to her mother. With the loss of her only girl, her helper and confidante, Mary grieved deeply, and played softly.

Although they had hoped for something more practical, the Ross family received a piano as a gift from Governor Dalhousie. (AUTHOR)

As decades passed, succeeding generations lost interest in the piano, and it was stored in a barn half buried in hay. As sons turned to hunting for sport as well as food, they saw nothing wrong with using strands of irreplaceable wire from the old piano to make rabbit snares. The piano lost its voice but killed a lot of rabbits.

In the mid-1900s, the piano was retrieved from the barn, restrung, and taken to the Nova Scotia Archives, where it was displayed for many years.

When Ross Farm Museum was formed in 1970, the piano was returned to Rosebank Cottage where, today, it stands in the parlour admired by Ross Farm Museum visitors.

WILLIAM THE ADMINISTRATOR

In addition to cutting a farm out of the forest, planting and harvesting his first crops, and building Rosebank Cottage and shelter for his animals, William had another challenge. As the senior officer, magistrate, and surveyor, he had to manage the affairs of the new settlement. He received a steady stream of orders, instructions, and replies from the governor's office. They came addressed to Lt. William Ross, Sherbrooke, and were hand delivered by any surveyor or governor official with other reasons to make the trip. As of 1818, the communications were addressed to Captain William Ross, signalling a promotion. Most of this correspondence was from his former commanding officer, Lieutenant Colonel M. Darling, who was by now the military secretary to Lieutenant Governor Dalhousie.

Darling kept all letters and documents, now in safekeeping at the Nova Scotia Archives in Halifax. One would wish that someone had been as careful with William's own letters, which have disappeared.

New settlers were arriving every month. William was ordered to assign them land and provisions.

"Lot for Frances Levy, late of Royal Artillery; Lot for Thomas Jeffety, Patrick Lawton, Edward Madden all late of Royal Artillery; Lot for John Tracey and Thomas Chives late of Nova Scotia Regiment."

One order William was glad to receive was: "Lot for McKay, the bearer of this letter, a blacksmith."

They needed a blacksmith badly.

William was asked for "a general plan of the settlement complete with the names of each soldier marked on the respective lots and a full report on those who have abandoned assigned land."

Then there were the provisions, which arrived in Chester by coastal vessel. In September 1817 supplies for sixty-one officers and men, fifteen women, and thirty-one children had to be transported to Sherbrooke, distributed, and documented. Sometimes the supplies were not of good quality, and their replacements came with a warning:

> Lord Dalhousie considers this a special bounty and Capt. Ross is to use his discretion. Distribution is to be made to the industrious and worthy only. Ross is to have the supplies conveyed to Sherbrooke as cheaply as possible and to guard against loss and waste; he is also to save some rations for future use.

It wasn't enough. The ration proved to be insufficient to tide them over. Two months later William wrote again for a further ration. Darling replied:

> The request for additional rations is unreasonable and I will not speak to Lord Dalhousie on the matter. Sherbrooke has been supplied 27

months instead of the promised 12. Sherbrooke has had two fine seasons and if they were not able to establish themselves by now, I doubt that they ever will. They have received extraordinary indulgence from the Government.

Put yourself in William's shoes, having to explain *that* to a hundred hungry people.

His Halifax masters were also stingy with respect to blankets. In February 1820, Darling wrote that settlers Johnson, Shaw, and Smith: "are to be given land and tools—but no blankets for new children. The Government will not allow this kind of waste."

The rations were terminated in October 1818.

Then there was the rum—ah, the rum. It was "the elixir that made pioneer life tolerable"; some were there for the rum alone. It was also a serious administrative problem for William Ross. An example: in December 1817, 485 gallons of two-thirds-proof rum was received and had to be distributed and accounted for. A month later in January when, apparently, some settlers had attempted to profit from selling rum rations (perhaps to buy blankets for their newborn?), William's suggestion to have rum removed from the rations was rejected as "too strong a measure." He was instructed to "exercise your authority as a Magistrate to prevent sale of rum without a licence."

In July 1818, Lord Dalhousie wrote to Captain Ross: "The rum ration is to be discontinued. You are to sell the remainder of the present supply, using proceeds to help settlers."

The free rum was no more, and many of the less stalwart settlers abandoned their holdings and left for Halifax, where rum was cheap and in good supply.

Medicines were also provided, although we know nothing of what kind. Lt. Col. Darling noted in his April, 1817 letter: "Lord Dalhousie wishes discretion in their distribution."

So William was also pharmacist for the community. Bibles were sent in March of 1817, though they did not arrive with instructions as to their distribution and use.

Also in March 1817, four hundred bushels of seed potatoes arrived. That was optimistic, as very little land had been cleared in that first late summer and fall. The potatoes would be planted the following summer between the stumps with a hoe. There was still no plow, which would have spared settlers' backs and allowed for earlier planting and better harvests.

Besides the allocation of land and the care and vittling of hundreds of people there was one ongoing concern—that road! The proposed road would link the settlement with Chester Basin, which was the shortest route to the South Shore, with its road to Lunenburg and coastal transport to Halifax. The next letter appointed William road commissioner and awarded a £100 grant for opening a road six feet in width from Gold River Bridge (just south of Ross Farm Museum) and the new settlement to what is now Charing Cross in the centre of New Ross. This was a major breakthrough.

Word of other farm and community advancements arrived. In April 1817, Darling promised "some choice grafted fruit trees."

Word came on February 24, 1818, that grant "assistance was forthcoming towards a mill."

December 1819: "a lot is set aside for a church."

But throughout all this correspondence with Lord Dalhousie's military secretary, Lieutenant Colonel Darling, something else emerges, another side of William Ross—his financial status. He and Mary must have been hard put to get by on his lieutenant's half-pay. In a letter dated November 17, 1819, Darling states: "There is little chance of Ross securing anything more than half-pay pension. The appointment in Windsor, in which you were interested, will probably go to someone else."

Was William considering and looking for a paying position outside the settlement? We will never know. We do know that he died intestate.

Darling also wrote that he thought "a plough would be useless in the present state of your territory." There is no record that a plow was ever provided.

Early life was not easy for settlers, who relied on animals for farm work and transportation. (ROSS FARM)

Despite differences about what was required for the struggling settlement, William and Darling had a good relationship. Mary and the children had been invited to the Darlings' home in Halifax, and Darling's letters were warm for the most part. Soon after, a letter arrived from Darling containing less than welcome news: "Lord Dalhousie has been appointed Governor of British North America, replacing Lord Sherbrooke in Quebec City."

And most remarkable of all was a letter from Mrs. Darling to Mrs. Mary Ross: "Thank you for your letter and your gift of earrings."

What was the relationship between Mary and Mrs. Darling? There she was, a pioneer woman in a sparse cottage in the Nova Scotia woods with no occasion to wear her wedding diamonds, giving them to a high-placed woman she seldom saw.

On June 2, 1820, Darling writes his farewell letter to William: "I will sail with Lord Dalhousie on the 4th for Quebec. Sir James Kempt will become the new Lieutenant Governor of Nova Scotia."

It is safe to say that whatever the relationship with Lord Dalhousie, William now had to deal with a new set of bosses. He received a letter in June 1820 from R. U. Howe, the newly appointed military secretary to Lieutenant Governor James Kempt. The parcel contained a supply of paper. Perhaps that was an indication of what was expected of William in the way of reports and applications.

Mary became concerned as she watched the ever-increasing demands take their toll on her husband. As industrious and dedicated as William was, he was wearing down.

THE END OF THE TRAIL

There was a threating sky on Monday morning, April 29, 1822, when William and Joseph, his Mi'kmaw friend and guide, set out to survey a route for the extension of the Old Military Road toward Hammonds Plains. Mary wondered if he should go. William had had a bad chest cold, sometimes with a fever, for the last two or three weeks, but he said, "I'll be fine, Mary. We should be home by dark."

William had his surveyor's compass and chain, and an axe. His guide carried an axe, his rifle, and the lunch that Mary had packed. It had been a typical Nova Scotia spring, cold and damp, and there was still snow in the woods. William had worked with Joseph many times and respected his native knowledge of the woods, with its game trails and hazards. But this was the first time they'd worked with a surveyor's chain, so William told him how to use it. Joseph set out, clearing the dense underbrush as he went, avoiding boulders, steep hills, and swamps, finding a way through the wilderness.

The first few miles were easy going, more or less following the path they'd walked for years. Then they came to a huge swamp, which could be crossed in dry weather but would be impassable year-round, so Joseph had to look for another way. In the late afternoon they heard thunder to the north, but they kept going. About seven o'clock it began to pour—a mixture of rain and sleet. Soon they were soaked.

William set out on foot on his final journey. Employees at the farm today honour the work ethic of the original settlers. (MATTHEW GATES)

William was feeling rotten, something like he had felt in Surinam when he thought he might be coming down with yellow fever. He had trouble breathing, and his chest hurt when he coughed. William and Joseph stopped for a rest.

Joseph brought William a drink of water, but he couldn't swallow. Could it be pneumonia, "the old man's friend"?

"But I'm not an old man, I'm not even forty," he thought.

Then it got dark and there was no hope of getting out of the woods until daylight. Joseph made a lean-to and a bed for William with branches. He covered William with his coat, but the shivering continued into the night.

Mary stayed up waiting for them.

At first light, Joseph got William to his feet, but he could barely stand. Then William's Mi'kmaw friend went for help. Sherwood was closest; he ran all the way and knocked on Captain Evans's door.

Four men followed Joseph back to the shelter where William lay, cut poles for a stretcher, and carried him to Sherwood. A bed was ready in Captain Evans's kitchen when they arrived, and William felt the warmth of the welcome and the fire, but the chills didn't stop. Captain Evans sent a young man through to Sherbrooke to tell Mary what had happened.

Next morning William was worse; his breathing was shallow and he couldn't stop coughing. Captain Evans arranged transport to Chester, where a doctor was waiting. "It's walking pneumonia," he told them. "There's a schooner sailing for Halifax at noon; it's his only chance." Joseph, William's loyal friend, returned to Sherbrooke to see if Mary needed help.

The wind was southerly and William's trip to Halifax was mercifully quick; they docked early next morning. But it was too late. William's non-stop labours of the past six years had exhausted his reserves, paving the way for pneumonia. He died on Thursday, May 2, 1822, at age thirty-nine.

The following week the *Acadian Recorder* (the principal Halifax newspaper) reported:

> DIED on Thursday last, Lieut. William Ross, on the half pay of the Nova Scotia Regiment and late of Sherwood Settlement. On Sunday his remains were interred with every demonstration of respect, the band and a firing party of the 81st Regiment attending; and His Excellency the Lieutenant Governor, the Commandant and Officers of the Garrison, and a number of Gentlemen of the town, followed him to the tomb.

How sad and incomplete was the obituary of this remarkable pioneer. He died away from home and Mary. Knowing that Mary was pregnant must have added torment to William's last days. He had promised to make Rosebank accessible by road. He died trying.

William Ross was buried among the noblemen of Halifax in what is now known as the Old Burying Ground. No records of the location of the grave exist, and no gravestone has been found.

We don't know whether Mary attended William's funeral. Mary's lot was difficult to imagine: a five months' pregnant widow with five young children and a few acres of cleared land in hundreds of acres of forest.

She applied for a widow's pension and was granted five pounds a year, plus one pound for each child. On September 9, 1822, her last son was born. She named him James Richard Uniacke Ross.

William's death at age thirty-nine left Mary with great responsibilities. He was buried in Halifax at the Old Burying Ground. (MURRAY CREED)

Rosebank Cottage was full of life, if not of worldly goods. Daughter Mary was now sixteen and helped with the baby. William, who had been born in Surinam and survived the shipwreck on the coast of Ireland, was now twelve. He helped feed the farm animals and split firewood to keep the cottage warm. Edward, who was born in England, was nine and was already helping with farm chores after school. George, who had been born in Lower Canada and who, like his brother Edward, had survived two shipwrecks, was seven. He fed the chickens and gathered eggs. Lawson, who was born in Sherbrooke, was four. With the baby, James, that made six children to feed, clothe, and nourish. Mary was now a widow with overwhelming responsibilities.

Livestock like these chickens are a big part of Ross Farm, which is known for its heritage breeds. (ROSS FARM)

CHAPTER FOUR

THE SECOND GENERATION

MARY WAS THIRTY-EIGHT WHEN SHE was widowed in 1822. Twelve years later, her sons had taken over the farm operation. Her daughter, Mary, was married to Andrew Kiens and lived across the lake with their four children and was pregnant with her fifth.

Mary's five sons all lived at home with her in 1834; Rosebank Cottage was a crowded, lively place. William, twenty-three, was married to Rachael Floyd of Chester, and they had two sons. He operated the family's gristmills and sawmills and was the community shoemaker.

Edward, twenty-one, who was born eight months after the Tuskar Rock shipwreck, was a storekeeper and trader. He also kept a diary of events on the farm and in the community, and of his own activities, especially his love life. Edward also helped with the farm work and kept the books for the farm and mill.

George, nineteen, born when his father was on garrison duty in Lower Canada, became the farmer. He married in 1831 and his line would inherit Ross Farm for generations to come. The younger sons, Lawson, seventeen, and James, thirteen, were still in school.

A few acres of land had been cleared, a barn built, and a well dug. They were still chopping down trees, burning land, and pulling stumps. They now had a few basic farm implements, including a single plow and homemade pin harrows

Mary and her children were left to work the land and care for all of the animals, which must have been daunting. (MATTHEW GATES)

fashioned by driving spikes into a crotch of a tree. It was hauled, as was almost everything else, by oxen.

There was still no road from Chester to Halifax.

Years later, Canada conducted its first census, which provides interesting facts about Ross Farm and those who lived there at that time. Ross Farm's 1871 census card lists residents, their ages, religion, and nationality. Mary was eighty-five (she and the family were listed as "Scotch"), her son, George, listed as head of the household, fifty-three, and his wife (also called Mary), thirty-eight. George and Mary's six children were named. One of these children, Albert, four, would later inherit the farm. A "servant," Augusta Seaborne, twenty-seven, and her daughter Florence, four, were listed as living at Ross Farm.

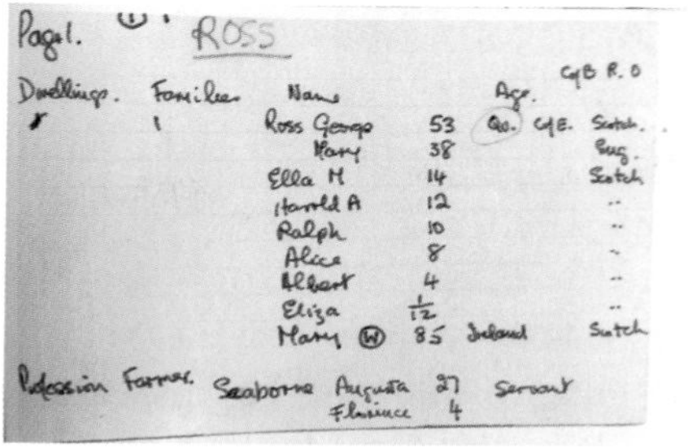

A census from 1871 shows the Ross family. (ROSS FARM)

A second census card listed three hundred acres farmed, two barns and stables, three acres of potatoes, four hundred acres of bush, one horse, four oxen, three milk-cows plus six young cattle, fifteen sheep, and two sows. The document said they produced two hundred pounds of butter and fifty pounds of cheese, plus forty pounds of wool and sixty-four pounds of flax fibre.

Mary, at eighty-five, must have been proud of what this second generation of Rosses had built on the foundation that she and William had laid down in this new land.

EDWARD'S DIARIES

William and Mary's second son, Edward, kept daily diaries for most of his eighty-one years, most of which are preserved at the

Nova Scotia Archives in their original form and on microfilm. He wrote in scribblers and notebooks, and often, when cramped for space, over-wrote across the page, resulting in difficult reading. His daily notes are the only first-hand account of life in Sherbrooke in that era, quoted by historians and storytellers. Many of these diaries were lost. Those that remain provide intimate details of the lives of pioneers in Nova Scotia.

The diaries came to light when Ross Farm Museum opened in 1970. Nova Scotia museum director J. Lynton Martin found the papers in Edward's old trunk in the Rosebank Cottage attic. As days passed, more diary pages turned up in nooks and crannies in the workshop and the haymow in the barn.

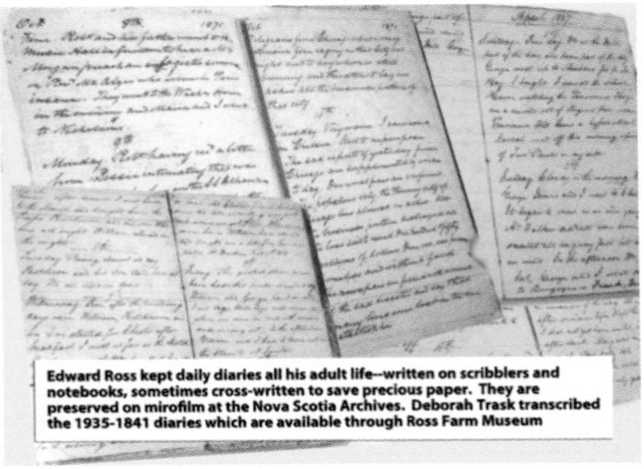

Deborah Trask, a museum director, archivist, and author, was commissioned to transcribe Edward's diaries for the years 1835 to 1841. The faded, blotched writings, some of which had been left in outbuildings for years, were a challenge to decipher. Pages were missing or torn as children of later generations read through them looking for the "juicy bits." There were many of these, as Edward was preoccupied with his own love life and that of his friends and neighbours.

Edward Ross kept daily diaries all his adult life--written on scribblers and notebooks, sometimes cross-written to save precious paper. They are preserved on mirofilm at the Nova Scotia Archives. Deborah Trask transcribed the 1935-1841 diaries which are available through Ross Farm Museum

Edward's diaries give insight into early life in and around the farm. Unfortunately, nothing written by Mary has been found, but we are left with these detailed entries by her son, who chronicled daily tasks and his love life. (AUTHOR)

His mother was the core of the family. There has been talk of a "sketch" Mary had written of her life, but that can't be found, so we must rely on Edward. His chronicles did not enter half of the daily activities on the farm—the woman's half. Edward mainly noted the weather, farm and mill work, his social and amorous affairs, his difficulties with credit, and stocking his little store.

The diary chronicles the tough times and repetitive labours. A luxury was a pint of rum. Hardship was a barn burning down in the night or a storm wiping out a sawmill that had taken months to build.

Typical of his diaries was his entry for December 24, 1835, in which he wrote that December was a month of unrelenting chores, butchering pigs and cutting up meat, cutting and hauling wood, banking the cellar with dung. Edward and his brothers cut wood right at the door into fireplace lengths and kept the fires in the kitchen and one of the upstairs bedrooms blazing. But it still didn't keep the potatoes in the cellar from freezing.

The potatoes were touched with frost. William built a fire in the cellar fireplace. They banked the cottage with snow and filled the cracks around the door with mud. Then it rained until Christmas Eve. That didn't stop the neighbours gathering around Edward's puncheon of rum. He then describes a fistfight that ensued:

> A real set-to, George and I trying to part the fighters, Rachael fainting, and Mamma and Mary crying, and trying to stop the fight. After a great ado, peace was restored with four left on the floor.
>
> After a while they all recovered and all went home—except George Driscoll. We did eat our supper and went to bed leaving him on the kitchen floor.

Christmas Day, Mamma apparently had had enough.

> We had not a morsel of bread, nor cake, nor a pudding this Christmas, for the first time in our lives. In fact, it appeared to me to be a dull Christmas altogether.

The rain continued to pour.

Those years on the farm were pedestrian in every sense; getting around was limited—you walked. On one occasion, Edward and his brother William walked thirty-five miles on a moose hunt, with no moose to show at the end of it. Edward regularly walked a radius of ten to twenty miles helping pensioners fill out forms for their pittance from the government. He walked behind the plow and in front of oxen hauling goods over terrible roads twenty-five miles to Chester. Getting enough exercise was not a problem.

In the fall of 1838, Edward and his younger brother Lawson set out on a ninety-five-mile walk through the hilly forest to Kentville and then down the Annapolis Valley to Cornwallis:

> Monday, September 28, Fine day. Lawson and I left home about half-past nine, for Cornwallis! We found the road long, tedious and lonesome. Lawson began to get very tired about 6 pm. We were recognized by Mr. Campbell who had slept at our house a few nights previous (though by the way he paid for it) and he asked us in.

It was common practice for travellers to knock on the door of a friend or acquaintance and ask for a drink of water as a hint, hoping for a meal or a bed for the night.

> I made the usual excuse "a drink of water if you please Mam" addressing the old dame. When I looked at her, I thought, "No lodging here for you young man." But I was agreeably deceived for when I enquired "How far to Kentville?" and made a motion to start, the old lady said, "you better stop to tea young man, and if you can put up with our accommodations, you are heartily welcome to stop all night." Such an offer at such a time of evening on a strange road was not to be rejected, weary and hungry from long fasting.

Next day, they walked to Kentville, stayed overnight before trudging down the Annapolis Valley to Annapolis.

Edward walked back to Sherbrooke alone, a 170-mile walk over five days—a three-hour trip today by car. One of his soles gave out and he had his boots repaired in Kentville.

EDWARD'S TRIP TO HALIFAX

Earlier that year, Edward made one of his frequent trips to Halifax—no small undertaking on foot to Chester and by sail to Halifax as there was still no road from Halifax to the South Shore.

He left home May 22, 1838, walked the fifteen miles to Chester Basin, and then took a five-mile dirt road to Chester where coastal boats called shallops sailed regularly to Halifax and back.

When the vessel was loaded (fourteen men and one cow) the wind swung southeast with driving rain, and nothing could get out of the harbour. The ship put the cow ashore to eat on the roadside while Edward bummed meals, drinks, and beds from friends and acquaintances. Five days later the weather changed. Edward describes the scene.

As the sun rose, the clouds cleared away and once more the glorious orb shed its benign rays over us poor sons of Mortality in a somewhat cheering manner. To my great satisfaction I saw the scud flying to the Eastward.

They scrambled to get the cow back on board.

We left the wharf at 9 A.M. We had not got to Ironbound (an Island in the Atlantic off the coast) ere the wind changed. We went into Dover and stayed the night.

Dover is a craggy inlet next to Peggy's Cove where they once again put the cow ashore to forage among the rocks. The men had no one to sponge off so they stayed on the boat.

Miserable bunks and worse beds, as to the eating, anyone who cannot eat anything at any time, under the influence of any smell, had better not go to sea. Skipper Barry dined ashore.

Five nights later they woke up to light westerlies, captured the cow again, and set sail for Halifax. They tied up at Fairbank's wharf that evening at sundown.

BY STAGECOACH TO WINDSOR

Edward had set his cap on becoming a magistrate. In May 1839, he writes about it in his diaries, beginning with his trip to Halifax:

> Called on the Provincial Secretary's office where I learnt that his Excellency the Governor was pleased to appoint me Justice of the Peace for the County of Lunenburg.

On July 3, Edward still had no confirmation of his appointment. He had waited long enough in his estimation.

> I am on my way to Halifax to find out the reason why I was not gazetted 'ere this. I got as far as Chester with my mare and wagon. We got on tolerably well until we came to a mud hole where the mare hauled both shafts out of the wagon and left us standing there. With the help of George Hiltz, soon got things arranged so far that I was enabled to proceed on my journey.
>
> Thursday, June 12, I went to the Secretary's office to enquire about my commission and Sir Rupert was very busy and could not attend to me then, but had wrote to the Judge (Haliburton) and had got no answer yet.
>
> I made up my mind to proceed to Windsor and have an interview with the Judge himself.

Edward met with another notable, William Lawson Jr., son of the man who had befriended the Ross family when they arrived in Halifax after the shipwreck in 1816. He very kindly drew up a letter to the judge and got it signed by three officials.

> July 4: I called into Shannon's and bought a nice hat and about 9 A.M. stepped into her Majesty's Mail Coach and was soon whirling along rapidly on my road to Windsor. I was the only passenger in the coach.

This stagecoach line from Halifax to Windsor was the first in Nova Scotia. It made its first run in February 1816, the year that Edward arrived in Halifax as a three-year-old boy. On the stagecoach trip to Windsor, the drivers and horses changed three times to avoid wearing out the horses and to get there in good time.

> The coach was very hot I therefore popped my head out the window, hailed the driver, and made him stop until I was seated alongside of him and then "crack" went the whip and we rolled along at the rate of 8 miles per hour around Bedford Basin. A fine refreshing breeze blew in my face and I could take a fine view of the country.

They passed Fort Sackville, Ten Mile House and Scott Manor House at the head of Bedford Basin, and drove on to the Fultz Inn, which was known as Twelve Mile House. At Twelve Mile House fresh horses were hitched to the coach and a new driver took over for another twelve-mile stage along the bumpy road to Windsor.

> The road itself was shamefully bad. As we entered the County of Hants the country improved.
>
> Cape Blomidon appeared in the distance covered with a gauze-like veil of haze, blended with the clouds in murky mistiness, like a gauze handkerchief thrown over a fair bosom of a beauty leaving the imagination to fancy more charms concealed beneath. We arrived in Windsor and immediately proceeded to the beautiful seat of T. C. Haliburton, the famed author of Sam Slick.

Edward was ushered into a sunlit room where he spotted a beautiful harp. There were stacks of books everywhere, not unusual for this man whose book *The Clockmaker* was acclaimed on both sides of the Atlantic and rivalled those of Charles Dickens.

As the grandson of a clockmaker, Edward must have been amused, when he picked up a copy of Judge Haliburton's book, to think that if his father had joined his grandfather's business instead of the British Army, Edward would probably never have been in this part of the world.

> After waiting awhile, Sam Slick himself entered. He was a man pretty well advanced in years, above the middle height of rather a

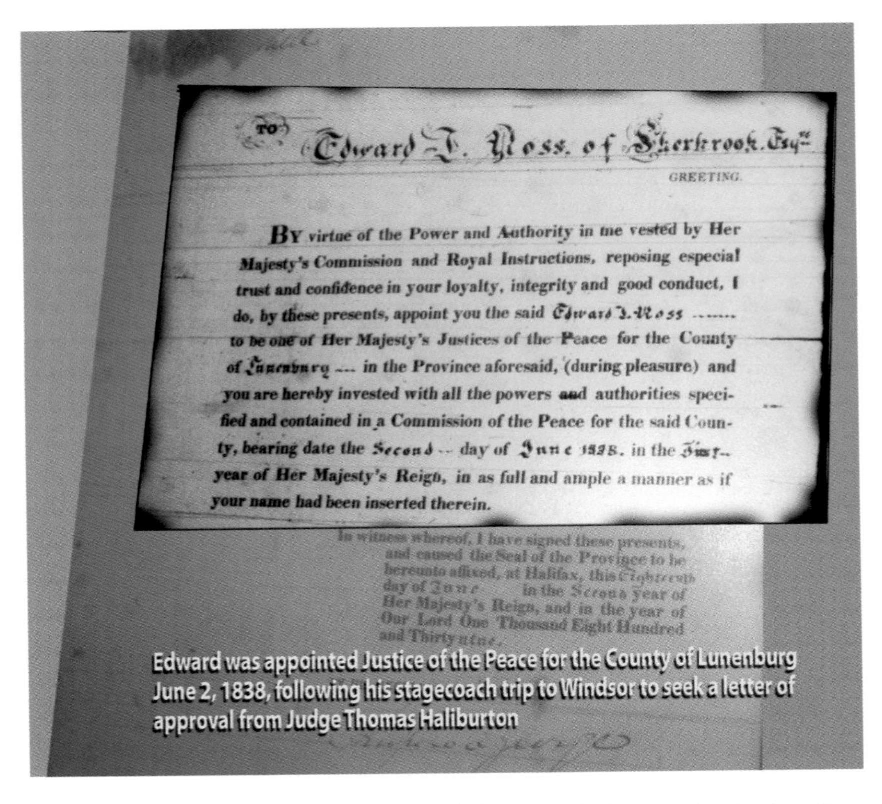

TO Edward J. Ross. of Sherbrooke. Esqr

GREETING.

BY virtue of the Power and Authority in me vested by Her Majesty's Commission and Royal Instructions, reposing especial trust and confidence in your loyalty, integrity and good conduct, I do, by these presents, appoint you the said Edward J. Ross ...... to be one of Her Majesty's Justices of the Peace for the County of Lunenburg --- in the Province aforesaid, (during pleasure) and you are hereby invested with all the powers and authorities specified and contained in a Commission of the Peace for the said County, bearing date the Second -- day of June 1838. in the First -- year of Her Majesty's Reign, in as full and ample a manner as if your name had been inserted therein.

In witness whereof, I have signed these presents, and caused the Seal of the Province to be hereunto affixed, at Halifax, this Eighteenth day of June in the Second year of Her Majesty's Reign, and in the year of Our Lord One Thousand Eight Hundred and Thirty nine.

Edward was appointed Justice of the Peace for the County of Lunenburg June 2, 1838, following his stagecoach trip to Windsor to seek a letter of approval from Judge Thomas Haliburton

Edward's goal was to become a justice of the peace. In his diaries, he describes that quest. (MURRAY CREED GRAPHIC)

> robust frame almost inclining to corpulence, the expression on his face rather haughty, a kind of aristocratic curl pervaded his mouth and nose which was slightly turned up (which by the way I have always remarked denoted impudence) but a fine forehead. When he entered the room he had a hat on his head and a cigar in his mouth. He addressed me with such politeness and when he had read the letter I had brought, he told me to leave and call again about 9 o'clock.

And so Edward was shown the door and wandered around the grounds. He admired the estate, walked across the Avon Bridge, paid a three-penny toll, and went out the gate to the streets of Windsor.

> At sundown I went to a hotel for some tea, and at 9 o'clock returned to Haliburton.

Finally, Judge Thomas Haliburton presented him with a letter to Sir Rupert, in which he confirmed Edward's appointment as justice of the peace for Lunenburg County, including Sherbrooke, the family home. Back at the hotel Edward wasn't in the mood to celebrate. A couple of acquaintances called with an abundance of brandy, but Edward dismissed them.

> I did not feel inclined for a debauch. I retired to bed.

On July 15, Edward was back on the coach and off to Halifax, where he hastened to the secretary's office. It was closed.

The next day, Sunday, Edward went to the Round Church, and on Monday he delivered Haliburton's letter. He was promised that his commission would be ready on Tuesday. Four days later he was in Lunenburg, paper in hand.

> On Saturday, June 22 I arrived to Lunenburg to take the Oath of Office, and my seat on the bench.

Edward was now an Officer of the Crown. His doggedness had paid off.

Great effort has been made to preserve the historical accuracy of the farm where Edward once lived. His diaries show him as a real person with strengths and weaknesses, successes and disappointments. (ROSS FARM)

TWO ROADS FROM ANNAPOLIS TO HALIFAX

Edward probably didn't realize it, but the road that the coach travelled to Windsor was in direct competition with the Old Military Road on which his home settlement was situated, the road that killed his father. There were two possible routes from Annapolis to Halifax, one through the woods and swamps on the rocky spine of Nova Scotia (where Sherbrooke lay), the other through the fertile Annapolis Valley.

The road Edward travelled to Windsor was the Valley route, and, even in those days, was passible, well used, and more practical.

At that time, the British controlled three forts—Fort Anne at Annapolis, Fort Edward at Windsor, and Fort Sackville at the head of the Bedford Basin. A road from these forts to Halifax was needed.

The Valley Road had an additional purpose; it was a drover's trail used to drive cattle, sheep, and hogs to market in Halifax. Huge herds walked this road to their fate at slaughterhouses and tanneries, which had sprung up on the edge of Halifax on Bedford Basin.

And then there was the "gentry" factor. Halifax society owned huge estates on the shores of Bedford Basin, where Prince Edward, lieutenant governors, and wealthy merchants had built palatial spreads along the water.

As a result, the military and the "money" both had good reason to develop the Valley Road as the preferred route to Annapolis. The other road through the rocky wilderness was the big looser. Its only supporters were settlers. It didn't have a chance.

ROSS'S MILL

In February 1818, Lieutenant Colonel Darling, military secretary to the governor, wrote to Captain Ross that Lord Dalhousie would be providing money toward the erection of a mill on an acre a short distance upstream on the Gold River.

For the early pioneers like William Ross, a sawmill was essential to escape the back-breaking labour of hewing logs into planks with a broad axe or sawing boards with a pit saw. A gristmill ground their wheat into flour, their barley into meal for the pigs, and their oats into oatmeal or rolled oats for porridge. They not only had to build those mills, they had to keep them operating—no small undertaking as they kept breaking down.

Oxen were critical to the operation of the farm. (MURRAY CREED)

The settlers hauled rocks and clay with ox teams, slowly dammed the river, and began to build their mills. A sawmill for lumber and a gristmill for grain. The water wheel, driven by the fast-running water of the mill race, turned at about 10 RPM, converted by a series of gears that would turn the grinding "runner stone" and the circular saw at many times that speed.

William, the oldest son, was the miller, while Edward and George helped out when needed and Edward kept the books. It seemed that they were constantly either repairing or rebuilding the gristmill and sawmill.

In the winter of 1835, William, George, and Edward spent many anxious nights at the mill worrying about ice jams, until on January 15 river ice broke the water wheel, which powered the mills. They decided to build a new mill and spent many days cutting and hewing timber for the sills and the frame. In early July, they framed up the sawmill. On August 6, they had a mill-raising party with plenty of grog, fiddling, and dancing.

On April 16, Edward writes:

> The rain fell in torrents all night and the spillway was swept away with the flood." Another big repair job was required.

Then on November 29, the mill burned down. Edward writes:

> All we could salvage were irons and nails; William was very much downhearted about the loss of the mill. In the language of the scripture, "He lifted up his voice and wept."

They began again cutting and hewing logs for the mill shaft and finished framing the gristmill.

On April 21, Edward writes,

> The grist mill was rose today.
>
> We had a Yankee Toss for six pints of rum.

April 21, 1838, was the day of the wedding that caused Edward to shout: "That's the last Baptist wedding that I will ever, ever go to. I was the Groomsman."

Edward was invited to a wedding in Chester on Christmas Eve, but there was no one to stand with the groom.

I was solicited to stand in and was ushered into the Bride's dressing room where the lovely young bride stood dressed for the occasion. She looked extremely well and as is quite natural on such occasions was all blushes and confusion. By this time word was sent to us that the company was assembled below and the clergyman was waiting so we descended to the parlour.

Anderson, the Groom was attired in a black frock coat with a white waistcoat and handkerchief and drab-coloured trousers. June Anderson officiated as Bridesmaid and the connubial knot was tied. The Bridegroom had strengthened himself with a couple of stiff glasses of gin and seemed stout hearted enough.

The females sat at the opposite side of the room. But the star of the company was the Bride who sat at the upper side of the room with her husband, her neck and face suffused with blushes.

I had formed a plan to get the Bridegroom intoxicated. I poured him a couple of glasses of raw brandy and persuaded him it was Port Wine. The butcher's wife spilt one cup of coffee on the carpet and then a cup of tea in her lap.

I toasted the Groom who sat next to me, and toasted him again, often and deeply. His eyes began to sparkle pretty briskly. Supper over dancing commenced. Mrs. Saunders sported he tall figure with the fat Mr. Schmitz. He whirled her about until her face glowed like a furnace and shone like a full August moon. David Crandall got so drunk that we had to carry him to bed. The butcher kissed his own wife—by mistake—and when their lips met it sounded like one of his steaks hitting the hot frying pan. I stayed up until midnight with the bridesmaid.

Oxen can still be seen on the farm. (MURRAY CREED)

It was a welcome reward for all their hard work.

Then they started on the gristmill. The gristmill began operating on October 1. The sawmill on October 12. Four days later, after a huge rainstorm, the dam was shaking, but Edward and his brothers hauled more rocks with the oxen and wagon to shore it up.

The next April, yet another rainstorm struck and part of the dam was washed out. And so dam building had to begin all over again.

EDWARD'S LOVE LIFE

One theme that ran though Edward's diaries was his fascination with girls. In the summer of 1835, Edward's diary took a personal turn. Louisa Russell's name popped up.

It was a Sunday afternoon. Edward had noted the sermon was "very good." After a visit to the Russells', Louisa, the daughter, walked back with him as far as Rosebank Bridge; they kissed and parted.

Mama came out and stopped us, accusing me of paying particular attention to Louisa. I got vexed and had cross words with Mother.

The following day, Edward, as was his habit, returned to writing details of the weather and farm chores when Louisa burst in with the news that a neighbour's calf had been killed by a bear that had jumped the fence. Edward and his brother, William, took off with a gun but "could not come up with it." That night, Edward went off to Russells' again. No word on what Mama thought of that.

On October 21, they were still digging potatoes. Edward did get a break. That evening he writes:

Louisa came in and I went home with her.

We had plenty of rum at my expense and kept up dancing until a late hour. Frank got drunk and lay on the kitchen floor all night. George and I went home with Johanna and Louisa. When we got near the house we seated ourselves on two rocks a little distance apart, paired and sat there towards daylight. We were driven home by a heavy shower and got a great drenching.

September 15: Danced and drank grog with Louisa.

16: Louisa is in my opinion a young woman of an excellent heart and disposition, and were she from her infancy removed from the influence of the rough course manners of her family, would be a credit to the world, a blessing to a good husband and an honour and ornament to society!

September 20: Went home with Louisa.

September 22: Spent the day with Louisa.

Edward's attraction to Louisa continued. In his mother's estimation, Louisa was not worthy of Edward. She was considered unsuitable for the son of a captain.

A flip back through the pages of the diary that autumn of 1835 makes it easy to see that Edward gave little thought to Mary's concern for his "station in life." In spite of his infrequent but valued contact with high society, and many flings with numerous women, Edward's relationship with Louisa lasted for many years, ending with her marriage to another man.

Edward married Maria Jane Barnaby in 1844 at age thirty-one, lived for several years in Boston, and returned to Kentville where he was Justice of the Peace for King's County. Rough years were ahead for Edward, as we will learn in later chapters.

MARY'S LONG LIFE

Mary's workworn life ended on July 31, 1876, at age ninety-two. She had survived her husband, William, by fifty-four years, and her daughter, Mary, by twelve years. All five of her sons were still living, and all but one attended Mary's funeral, in addition to dozens of grandchildren, and great-grandchildren. A new Anglican church had just been built in New Ross where the funeral took place. She was buried in the old Anglican cemetery. Her eldest son, William, was to die three months later in Cornwallis.

Mary had seen Sherbrooke renamed New Ross thirteen years earlier, in 1863; the primitive settlement she helped William found in 1816 was now a thriving farming and lumbering-based community.

Flowers bloom on the farm where Mary lived until she was ninety-two. (MATTHEW GATES)

She lived to see Confederation in 1867, the centennial of which provided the impetus for starting Ross Farm Museum.

Alexander Graham Bell had patented the telephone earlier in the year she died. She would never use one. Nor would she live to see rural mail delivery, electric lights, or rubber-tired wagons. Eaton's catalogue, full of household goods, which came out eight years after her death in 1884, could have made her isolated life easier.

Transportation had made massive advancements in Mary's lifetime. Ocean-going square-rigged ships had been replaced by steamships, cutting Atlantic travel time from months to a week or two. How she would have enjoyed shorter travel times when she and William sailed to and from Surinam and across to Quebec! And perhaps they would have avoided two shipwrecks.

Acres owned 300 75 IM. 25 Pas. 1 gar.
Barns & Stables 2
carriages & sleighs 2
carts waggons & sleds 2
Boat 1
ploughs & cultivators 1
Fanning mill 1

Horses 3+ 1
W Ox 4
M. Cow 3
Ot H C 6
Sheep 15
Sw 2

½ wheat - 10 bus sp. wh.
15 bus barley.
40 bus oats
7 b. rye
3 b. beans
10 b. buckwheat
3 acres potatoes 400 bush.
80 b. turnips other 5
50 b carrots & other

Hay. 20 acres
30 tons.

Butter 200
cheese 50
wool 40
Fabric 64

Old documents like this census card for Ross Farm give snapshots of the early days on the farm. (ROSS FARM)

Farm animals have always been an important part of the Ross Farm story.
(MATTHEW GATES)

CHAPTER FIVE

THE THIRD AND FOURTH GENERATIONS

GEORGE ROSS, WHO LIVED OUT the 1800s as the family head of Ross Farm, died there in 1903 at age eighty-seven. He was buried in the Old Anglican Cemetery in New Ross.

His fifth son, Albert, who was unmarried, took over the farm in 1903 and lived at Rosebank Cottage with his spinster sister, Lizzie. The son of one of their sisters, Ethel, would inherit Ross Farm after Albert and Lizzie died.

Albert, known as "the second Captain Ross," joined the militia as captain in 1889 and retired in 1913 as lieutenant colonel. The military tradition had carried on through another generation.

The road from Sherbrooke to Hammonds Plains had still not been built but there was a passible road to Chester Basin and to Kentville. A road had been pushed through along the South Shore from Chester to Halifax, making the slow journey by water a thing of the past.

In Albert's time, the pioneering phase of Ross Farm was over, small mixed farming had begun, and life was comfortable though money was scarce.

Gradually, manufactured implements and farm machinery became available and—as farmers were able pay for it—marvellous new labour-saving devices began to appear in the community and in Eaton's catalogue.

In 1834, the horse-drawn reaper, invented by Cyrus McCormick, made grain harvesting easier, with back-and-forth

Inventions like the kerosene engine changed life on the farm. (AUTHOR)

cutting blades and flailing arms that swept clumps of cut grain onto the field—to be gathered up and bound into sheaves.

It was succeeded by the binder in 1872, which cut and bound the grain into sheaves, which women and older children stood up in the field to dry in "stooks" of eight.

The dried sheaves of grain were cut open and beaten against the barn floor with a flail, knocking the grain off the straw. Then came the thrashing machine powered by a horse treadmill or a gasoline engine, which was moved from farm to farm where neighbours gathered to do the thrashing in one day—always with a big meal served by the ladies to the dusty, hungry men at midday. That evening they would have a barn dance, if there was a fiddler in the thrashing crew.

But the most revolutionary change was yet to come—the internal combustion engine.

The first farm engines didn't propel vehicles or haul tillage equipment. They were simple "one-lunger" stationary engines that pumped water, turned circular saws, and performed a host of other tasks. The same engines, made in Lunenburg and mounted on schooner decks, hoisted sails and ran bilge pumps. Then in the 1930s came the real game-changer—the tractor—which brought with it bigger, heavier, cultivation and harvesting equipment. But ox and horsepower prevailed, and there was never a tractor on Ross Farm.

Captain Albert Ross died at home in 1950, his sister, Lizzie, three years later, and Ross Farm was passed to the fourth generation, Ross White, the son of their sister, Ethel. With that act, the White name appeared on the Ross Farm deed and continues to today.

THE STRANGER WITH THE FLUTE

One autumn day twenty years after his father's death, George Ross was clearing land down by the Gold River when he spotted a man approaching him from downstream, stopping every few feet and turning over a rock.

William called out, "Good morning sir! I'm George Ross, and what would be your name?"

"Abraham Gesner," he replied. "I'm a geologist by calling, a medical doctor by profession, and an inventor by choice. It's been quite a walk over the hills from the Valley; I was collecting rock samples along the river bank, looking for coal, in fact."

Slowly, at supper, the stranger's story came out. Abraham Gesner was indeed a medical doctor and a surgeon, educated in England, and practising in Horton (which later became Kentville). His studies included geology and mineralogy, and he had made a study of the land formations in Nova Scotia, New Brunswick, and Prince Edward Island.

And of even more interest to William, he played the flute and fiddle and loved Old Country music. Albert went to his rucksack and pulled out his flute, William picked up his fiddle, and they struck up "The Road to the Isles."

He stayed overnight. Edward was in Halifax, and his bed was available. Next morning Gesner moved on. Edward returned from Halifax with a copy of the *Acadian Recorder* and they learned more about Abraham Gesner:

GESNER INVENTS NEW LAMP OIL—KEROSENE
CITADEL HILL FORTRESS LIGHED BY OIL LAMP
SUSPENDED ON SIGNAL ARM
TO DELIGHT OF ALL ASSEMBLED.

Gesner's kerosene would replace whale oil and change lives as this new oil made the winter nights brighter—lamps for kitchen and bedrooms, lanterns for the barn and mill and for those necessary trips to the outhouse.

Gesner has been said to have saved more whales than Greenpeace.

EDWARD AGAIN

Edward's diary-keeping continued until his death. Twenty years after his marriage in 1844, he and his wife moved to Port Medway.

> April 14, 1868: It is a hard time for me to be detained here in Port Medway in debt, which I never contracted.
>
> June 3, 1868: 55 today, in debt, and my home has slipped away from my grasp.
>
> February 11, 1889: My ready cash is reduced to the magnificent sum of 10 cents.
>
> June 5: Alas, I have no permanent home. My mind is tossed on a fearful sea of doubts and perplexities. I cannot make up whether to go to Halifax or Boston. To one place or other I must go, and that soon.
>
> October 16, 1869: Oh, why can I not get some profitable employment? My clothes are getting shabby, my shoes are wearing out, and I see, as yet, no means of replacing them.

Two years later, back in New Ross on New Year's Day, he wrote:

> I am here out of employment, the guest of my brother George. My poor wife is in Boston.

Debts adding up, Edward decided to go to Boston to look for work.

He travelled to Kentville where he stayed overnight with his brother William before proceeding to Margaretsville and boarding the schooner *Talisman* to Boston.

Five weeks later, he had landed a job selling subscriptions for a monthly publication called *Merry's Museum*—probably on commission.

His first real job was as a bookkeeper at two dollars a day. Three years later, he was hired as warehouse-factory night watchman and given a small office space from which to begin an import/export business—shipping onions and other goods to Halifax.

> September 23: Received a letter from J. W. Horseman saying "sending a barrel of potatoes with 5 bottles of brandy inside...dangerous experiment ... Would not wish to be detected smuggling. I hope the shipment is not seized in transit.

Then there came health troubles.

> November 16, 1874: Maria's liver is afflicted and I feel very uneasy about her.

On July 31, 1876, his mother, Mary, died "of general disability," and four months later his oldest brother, William, died.

> April 30, 1881: I was taken with deafness this morning.
> September 25, 1882: Messenger rushed up with the shocking news that my wife was violently ill. "If you want to see your wife alive you had better hurry down." When I reached the house she was too far gone to speak, and fell asleep, calm as a baby with her dear hand in mine. Words fail to describe my grief.
> September 27: With my beloved wife in her coffin.
> September 28: The funeral took place at 1 p.m. The church was crowded and a large crowd followed my beloved's remains to the last resting place in Oak's Cemetery, Kentville. No home for me now, my effects will all be scattered. I must seek an alternate abode somewhere else.

He moved home and is listed in the 1891 census as living at Rosebank Cottage where he died on April 8, 1894, at eighty-one.

Of all his siblings, only his brother George outlived him, dying in 1903.

THE FOURTH GENERATION

When Lizzie Ross died childless in 1953, her obituary in the *Windsor Tribune* mentions that her only sister, Mrs. Ethel White of Windsor, had been caring for her during the last several weeks. Ethel was the wife of Rev. Charles White. Their son, Mark, who was married to Nina Keddy and had served overseas in the Second World War, inherited Ross Farm.

The White family moved in to Rosebank Cottage and raised a family of eight children. The farm had begun to decline in the preceding generation as Albert grew older and couldn't keep up with the changes in farming that were sweeping the country. Mark White struggled to bring it back to its former productive state. Then in 1963 he died early, leaving his widow, Nina, the burden of raising a young family and running the farm. Nina, like many farm women of the time, was forced to seek off-farm work.

In the late 1960s, it became clear to Nina that she could no longer maintain Ross Farm as a viable operation. Then she had an idea—donate Rosebank Cottage and a sizable portion of the land to the people of Nova Scotia as a living farm museum to honour its founders, William and Mary Ross, and help preserve the tradition and values of the pioneers. The timing of her decision couldn't have been better, as the community was looking for a way to celebrate Canada's centennial. Things started to happen in 1969.

CHAPTER SIX

ROSS FARM MUSEUM

THREE CONTRIBUTING FACTORS LED TO the founding of Ross Farm Museum: the 150th anniversary of Ross Farm in 1966, the centennial of the Confederation of Canada in 1967, and a collection of early farm machinery that needed a home. Committees were formed in New Ross in 1963 to find a way to satisfy these needs. The consensus was: create a museum.

In 1969, Nina White offered Rosebank Cottage and a portion of Ross Farm to the government of Nova Scotia as a home for an historic farm museum. Ron Barkhouse, a storeowner

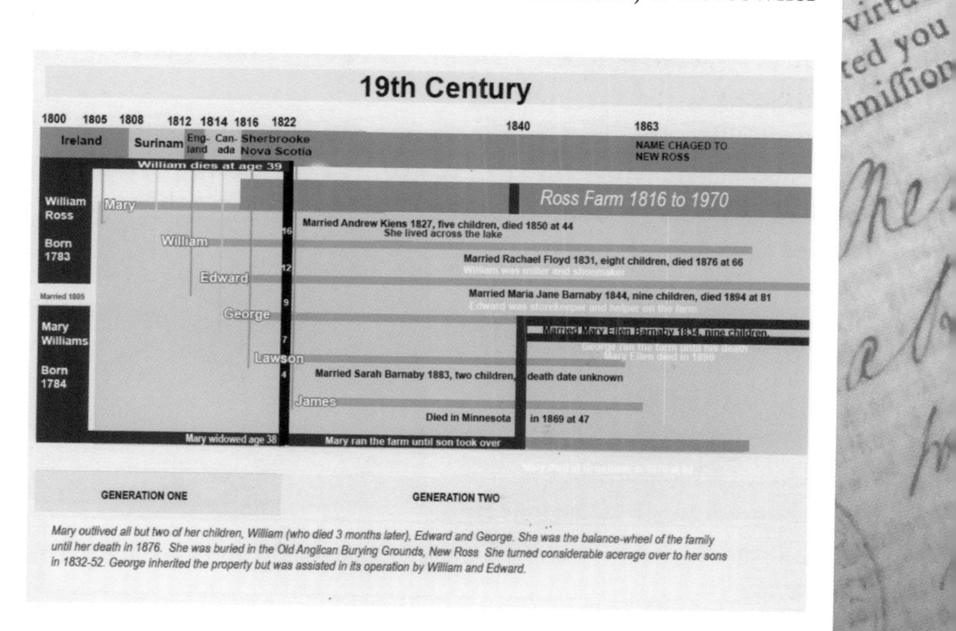

A Ross family tree. (MURRAY CREED GRAPHIC)

and sawmill operator in New Ross, became president of the newly formed Ross Farm Museum, and J. Lynton Martin, director of museums for Nova Scotia, who had assembled an extensive collection of early farm machinery, took charge of establishing the farm as a museum. Nina White became assistant curator and later was elected president.

The first act was to hire a competent person to turn the farm property into a museum. Allan Hiltz, a local farmer and 4-H leader, was hired as curator in 1969, and he and his wife, Bernice, moved into the building that later housed the gift shop and offices. He managed the museum for over thirty years until he retired in 2000.

Ross Farm Museum was opened to the public August 7, 1971, and was a success from day one. Only nine years later, on August 9, 1980, the museum welcomed its 500,000th visitor, a Mrs. Alger of Riley Ville, Virginia.

When the museum began, the buildings needed renovation and there were no livestock on the farm. Allan Hiltz bought a pair of oxen in 1969—the first animals at Ross Farm Museum—and used them to plow the first furrow.

In 1990, the first heritage breed animal was introduced to Ross Farm Museum—the Canadian Horse imported from Quebec. In succeeding years, other heritage breeds, livestock that originated in a bygone era, were added, including Berkshire pigs, Southdown and Cotswold sheep, and half a dozen historic breeds of chicken and geese.

Staff member with a Canadian Horse, the first heritage breed on Ross Farm. (ROSS FARM)

Schoolchildren come by bus to enjoy hands-on experiences in the barns and historic kitchen in Rosebank Cottage.

The 4-H motto, "Learn to Do by Doing," in Allan's background and his approach soon paid off. With no formal training in museum management, he brought his farmer's ingenuity, inventiveness, optimism, common sense, and determination to the job, along with a rare gift of showmanship. As he said:

> Our museum is a stage. We perform a play every day. As people get out of their cars, things happen; ox bells ring as they haul logs out of the woods, people make hay in the meadow, a child brings a drink of cold water down to them, women bake bannock in the fireplace. It's all part of the scene of life on a working farm.

Staff members bring warmth and a friendly welcome to Ross Farm Museum visitors, just like guests in their own homes. Most come from the community, bringing with them time-honoured skills and craftsmanship, and they wear the clothes of the 1800s, made in the museum.

These are practical people who reflect the values and skills of the men and women who came before them. They raise and care for the animals; they plant, harvest, and cure crops, and carry on homemaking in Rosebank Cottage, using the tools and equipment of the 1800s.

They repair farm equipment and farm buildings. Coopers make barrels, craftsmen make snowshoes and spoons in the workshop, and blacksmiths shoe oxen in the forge. Candles and soap, and clothes from farm-grown flax and wool are made in the cottage. The Pedlar's Shop sells products made on Ross Farm, including fireplace tools, maple bowls turned from farm tree burls, and fine needlework.

Ross Farm Museum became one of the few museums outside Halifax to be open in the winter. It made good sense as the farm was operated year-round and farm work doesn't end with the summer tourist season.

When Allan Hiltz retired to his own farm in 2000, Ross Farm Museum had well-established heritage breeds of horses, hogs, sheep, and poultry, teams of oxen, and a modest cropping program worked by animal rather than tractor power. A working blacksmith's shop provided one of the few ox-shoeing services in the province, and a cooperage turned out tubs and barrels for sale. Numerous hands-on programs were underway, including a very popular pumpkin-growing program for kids where seeds were planted in the spring and each child returned to Ross Farm Museum in the fall to harvest his or her very own pumpkin. An ambitious program of visitor and community activities had been established and the museum had attracted visitors from all over Canada, the United States, and many European countries. Ross Farm Museum was a success—perhaps too much so. Its building would no longer accommodate all its activities. The next millennium would address that shortcoming.

THE CANADIAN HORSE

When Allan Hiltz brought the first breeding animals of the heritage breed to Ross Farm Museum, he began a program that has become one of the farm's most important features.

First came the Canadian Horse, a distinctive breed, established in the late seventeenth century in Quebec from the stables of Louis XIV in France. The resulting horse is muscular, compact and stout, noted for soundness, hardiness, and endurance.

The horses thrived and were nicknamed "the little iron horse" and "the horse of steel." By 1763, there were around thirteen thousand Canadian Horses in Lower Canada (Quebec).

Later, thousands of horses were exported to the United States, for both the Civil War and as breeding stock for the growing stagecoach lines.

On April 30, 2002, the Canadian Horse was named an official symbol of Canada, along with the Mounties and the beaver.

Horses are shown here on the farm in winter. The Canadian Horse is noted for stamina and a team can get you places at a fast clip. (ROSS FARM)

In March 1990, Allan Hiltz bought two Canadian Horse mares-with-foal in Quebec. The two colts were born at Ross Farm, and one was raised there. Hiltz later bought a stallion in Quebec, and the progeny of these first three animals are still at Ross Farm Museum.

HERITAGE HOGS AND SHEEP

Next, Hiltz went to Ontario and bought breeding stock of Berkshire pigs, known for their hardiness and marbled meat.

Berkshire pigs are said to be "Britain's oldest pig breed," discovered by Cromwell's troops during the English Civil War. Today's animals descend from the herd maintained by British monarchs since the early eighteenth century; its pork is prized for juiciness, flavour, and tenderness.

Then came heritage breeds of sheep—Cotswold and Southdown. The Cotswold breed was already in Britain when the

Normans invaded. It was nicknamed the "Golden Fleece Breed," yielding the fabulous cloth of gold of antiquity.

Cotswold wool was used as a substitute for linen, woven with exceedingly fine wires of real gold, to make special garments for ancient priests and kings as described in the Bible. As far back as the thirteenth century, Florentine merchants travelled to England and bought large quantities of the shiny, linen-like wool.

It is also known as "no itch," and is often been called "poor man's mohair," and the curly locks are often sold as Santa Claus beard material.

The Southdown is a small, dual-purpose British sheep, raised primarily for meat. Originally bred about two hundred years ago, it has recently been placed on the watch list by the Rare Breeds Survival Trust. The original Southdown breed reached North America in 1803. They were known as the "Aberdeen Angus" of the sheep industry for their compact carcass, which was reminiscent of that of the Angus beef cattle breed. This small breed was sometimes called "Babydoll" and became a popular 4-H show animal. Ross Farm's collection of heritage animals continues to grow.

HERITAGE POULTRY

Heritage poultry were added later—Silver Gray Dorking and Silver Spangled Hamburg chickens, Muscovy ducks, and Embden geese.

The five-toed Silver Gray Dorking is an ancient breed named for the southern English town Dorking. The Romans brought these five-toed fowl with them when they invaded Britain in AD 43.

The Hamburg breed of chicken was developed in Germany and the Netherlands prior to 1700. It is a small breed capable of flight.

HERITAGE DUCKS

Muscovy ducks had been domesticated in the Americas when Columbus arrived. They are widely traded as "Barbary duck" with their stronger-tasting meat—sometimes compared to roasted beef—or as "quackless duck" as they don't actually quack (except in cases of extreme stress).

Muscovy ducks are also worth their weight in gold, eating mosquito larvae in the water and on the wing. They eat flies and maggots and do a lot to keep the fly population down. They also love roaches and eat them like candy.

HERITAGE GEESE

Embden geese are effective weeders because they like grasses but not most broadleaf plants like strawberries. They cut down on hoeing and help avoid using herbicides.

Heritage breeds all make their contributions to Ross Farm—horse power in the fields, wool for knitters, meat for the table, weeding for the garden, and insect control for the barnyard. And at the same time, these often overlooked breeds are promoted and preserved.

FLAX

Sheep's wool comes to mind when we think of homegrown farm clothing, but there was another important source in early Nova Scotia pioneering days—flax. That was true in William and Mary's time and for several generations after.

Edward referred to flax planting, harvesting, breaking, and spinning throughout his early diaries, and those activities are still carried out at Ross Farm Museum.

With their Irish roots, William and Mary remembered that flax was the one important cash crop of Irish farmers. The sails that

propelled them from Ireland to Surinam, back to Ireland, to Canada, and to Nova Scotia were made of linen; and linen was the everyday fabric of the clothing they wore.

Nearly sixty thousand Irish farmers were registered with the Irish Linen Board in 1796. It was known as the Spinning Wheel list or the Flax Growers Bounty, providing spinning wheels and looms based on the number of acres of flax planted. One acre yielded four spinning wheels and five also provided a loom. No Ross or Williams families were on the list (which is not surprising as they were upper-class city people).

One hundred days after planting, the flax stems were pulled from their roots (not cut, so that every inch of the stem was retained.) Flax stems were bundled together into sheaves (called beets) before being carried in carts to fields where women and girls would spread them into stacks called stooks to dry in the sun.

Flax drying in the field before breaking and being woven into linen. (ROSS FARM)

Then came the nastiest part of the process that transforms the flax plant into beautiful cloth: retting. Retting is the process of rotting away the inner stalk using bacteria, leaving the outer fibres intact.

After ten days, the retted flax could be removed from the pond. It was hard and unpleasant work lifting the heavy, sodden, stinking mess.

Traditional bleaching methods included boiling the cloth in a solution of water and ashes, seaweed, or fermented bran. The cloth was then rinsed and spread over an area of grass (bleach greens) to dry in the sun. It was repeatedly steeped in buttermilk, rinsed, and spread out again.

The cloth was given at least twelve boilings in a witch's brew of cow's urine, cow dung, buttermilk, potash, bran, and salt. The cloth was then spread on grass to dry, after which it was again watered, dried, and then hammered on a flat stone with a wooden mallet or beetle.

William's friend and military colleague, James Wells, was engaged as schoolteacher the year the settlers arrived, and taught the children in his home across Lake Lawson until 1818, when £100 was allocated to build a school. Many one-room schools were built throughout the district in the 1800s.

The one-room schoolhouse was moved to the Ross Farm property and is now an important teaching tool. (MURRAY CREED)

In the 1960s, when New Ross was considering centennial projects, one of the possibilities was to acquire and preserve a one-room school. When the priority switched to founding Ross Farm Museum, a one-room school was later added to the property, when Ron Barkhouse and a few co-conspirators hauled a one-room school building from Harriston, near Kentville. (The story goes that they hauled it by night with farm tractors because they had no highway permits.)

Today's schoolchildren enjoy visiting the one-room schoolhouse at Ross Farm Museum, which is situated close to the large flat rock where Capt. William Ross probably spread out the settlement plan and allocated plots of land to his fellow Sherbrooke settlers.

In addition to the thousands of children who visit Ross Farm Museum with their parents, tens of thousands more arrive each year with their teachers by school bus.

Over a quarter-million students from as far away as Cape Breton have taken part in the school program since it was instituted in 1971.

A visit to Ross Farm Museum is now part of school curriculum. Children who have taken part in this school program now bring their own children to experience the museum and what it represents.

School visits include hands-on learning with open-hearth cooking, candle making, blacksmithing, woodworking, and wool processing from sheep to yarn. Students feed farm animals and go on guided nature walks. They experience classroom life in a century-old school using quill pens (made from Ross Farm rooster feathers) and slate boards and chalk. It's a fun day!

Back at school, the learning continues, based on things seen and done on Ross Farm. Follow-up studies include: Where does food come from? How has cooking changed? Who cares for our earth?

NEW ROSS THEN AND NOW

If William and Mary Ross could have looked ahead two centuries, they would be amazed, and perhaps just a little dismayed, at how the settlement has struggled, flowered, and faded in those two hundred years, and is about to bloom again with the construction of a $3-million Learning Centre on the farm they pioneered.

The area's chief exports (in addition to young people seeking broader opportunities) have progressed through barrels, lumber, and Christmas trees to wind-generated electricity in the South Canoe thirty-four-turbine wind farm. The cold winter winds that froze the settler's faces and the summer zephyrs that dried their meadow hay will now generate electricity that will flow over copper wires to help power thirty-two thousand homes in nearby Nova Scotia towns and villages.

Many of the most telling developments are now recalled through scrapbooks, local histories, and fading memories of the oldest of the community's citizens. The annals of the New Ross Historical Society provide photographic and written records of the ever-changing conditions and times.

Ron Barkhouse provided facts, insights, and observations in his booklet, *The Olden Days and the Olden Ways*. In his Halifax home a few months before his death in the spring of 2014, he shared his memories of New Ross.

Ron told us: "The road to Chester Basin might have been built about 1820—it was little more than a path then—but when it was extended past New Ross to Kentville (which was once considered an impossible task) it became the lifeline connecting the settlement to the South Shore and to the Annapolis Valley."

Ron writes that another road, the New Russell Road, which ran cross-country from Charing Cross to Vaughan on the Chester-Windsor road, was declared passable in 1863. It became the eastward extension of the Forties Road and skirted the hilly, swampy terrain to the south where the Old Military Road would have run and where William died in a failed attempt to find a passable way through.

As the road to Chester Basin was gradually widened and improved, ox teams hauled essentials to and from the South Shore and later to the Annapolis Valley. Highway 12 through New Ross from Chester Basin to Kentville has become the principal route from New Ross to the rest of Nova Scotia—"Up through" to the Annapolis Valley and "outside" to the South Shore.

The motor vehicle changed everything when it was introduced in the early 1900s. The older residents of New Ross and vicinity remember the first cars. They recall the dates through events in their own lives, and many have scrapbooks to back up fading memories.

For Shirley Hiltz it was the story of her parent's wedding: "My mother and father married in 1925 and they drove a Model T Ford and they drove to the Forties and back and that was their honeymoon. That was a big outing, all of five or ten miles." She also remembers that her mother and her bridesmaid were wearing the same hat they each had picked from the T. Eaton catalogue.

The telephone came to the community in 1906, Ron Barkhouse notes, and people got the news and gossip from party-liners all over the community—everyone listened in on the calls until the signal was so weak they were told to hang up. And even then, many just held down the receiver for a second and continued to listen in. Electricity came in 1946. Bernice Hiltz remembers the date by two events, her wedding day and her brother's death.

"We had power. We had lights. We had everything. I was all excited because I was going to get married! And I could get married in the church because there would be lights there—wouldn't have to use those old lamps. But it had a very sad sequel. About two weeks after we were married, there was a power failure and my brother, Otis, who was twenty-six and just back from overseas, went to help my brother-in-law, who was in charge of electricity in New Ross, fix the line. He climbed up the pole and something happened and he was electrocuted and died right there."

Ron Barkhouse writes that with the coming of power and motorized vehicles, New Ross developed and prospered despite the absence of water or rail transportation or good roads. It had three general stores, a hardware store, auto and machinery repair shops, a steam mill—even a funeral parlour. But fire took its toll. In 1918, the Foresters Hall, Lohnes Hall, Al Lohnes Funeral Parlor, Parnell Gates Barbershop, and Scott Barkhouse's residence were lost.

In 1946, the New Ross Fire Department was formed, but still several stores were destroyed in 1967.

Christmas-tree production has become a major contributor to the economy of New Ross and the area. The Nova Scotia Christmas tree industry peaked in 1957 at 3.8 million trees, centered in the New Ross area with its own production research

BARRELS

Much of the prosperity of New Ross came not from farms but from the forest and one of its by-products—barrels.

Barrels were an important export in New Ross. (ROSS FARM)

Nova Scotia's first barrel production dates back to 1863 when Daniel O'Neil fashioned one from heat-bent spruce staves and sapling hoops. His no-cost materials grew abundantly right outside his door, his methods were easy for others to master, and 122 cooperage shops sprang up in New Ross and vicinity.

These barrels were shipped by ox–hauled wagon, some to the South Shore for the fishery, and most to the Annapolis Valley for the apple-export business. This two-day oxen haul was replaced by one-hour truck transport of three hundred barrels daily to the Annapolis Valley where they were packed with fruit and shipped to Britain.

Ross Farm Museum has a working cooperage, which turns out barrels, kegs, and buckets for sale in the gift shop and for special orders, including fifty wooden buckets for the Hollywood movie *McCabe & Mrs. Miller*, for a church-fire scene where the hero (played by Warren Beatty) is hiding out from killers.

program. However, in recent years, shipments have declined, faced with increased competition from US-grown and artificial trees.

The early trees weren't much like today's trees, remembers Shirley Veinot. "They were tinsel trees—loaded with store-bought icicles." Today, Christmas-tree growers prune, thin, and fertilize their trees, producing the perfectly formed dense specimens that are shipped all over the world, allowing Lunenburg County highway signs to boast—Balsam Fir Christmas Tree Capital of the World.

Medical help has always been hard to get in New Ross. For many years the doctor had to come from Chester or Kentville and was seldom called before the sick person was extremely sick—sometimes too late. No doctor was willing to move to New Ross until the 1940s when the Farmers Association built a doctor's house to sweeten the pot. Shirley Veinot remembers that the resident doctor left in the late 1960s.

New Ross still has no drugstore, so prescriptions must be picked up on the South Shore or in the Annapolis Valley. "When you live in a rural community you have to plan," said Evelyn Hiltz.

All local banking is done through the only financial institution, the New Ross Credit Union, which also boasts an ATM.

Perhaps the most significant local change in community life occurred when the ten district one-and two-room schools were replaced by the New Ross Consolidated School on Highway 12 and children were bussed in. Community life had centred around these schools and, with their closing, the sense of community suffered. The new consolidated school did something else. It prepared its students for outside opportunities, and the young people moved away. "It's bittersweet," says Evelyn Hiltz, who returned from a teaching career in Newfoundland and Labrador to be with her mother, Bernice. "It's great to have young people educated, but it's been a turning point as far as keeping people here."

Some of these little schools are still around today, put to other uses. The Forties School was converted into a community hall and community centre. Harriston School, as we learned earlier, was hauled to Ross Farm Museum where it is visited by thousands every year.

Ross Farm is more popular than ever with visitors. (ROSS FARM)

Agriculture is changing too. "Used to be a lot of family farms, but now you could easily count them on two hands," Kathy Hiltz told us. She is a director of Ross Farm Museum, and her husband operates a farm on the Forties Road, and commutes to his engineering firm in the Annapolis Valley. "When the district schools went they lost the sense of small community; now they're in the world of Internet. We're still a very social bunch—we like to get together, our churches (small as they are) are still active." But New Ross, like most Nova Scotia rural communities is struggling. "People commute to work in Halifax, the Annapolis Valley, and the South Shore. We're becoming a mecca for senior citizens," Hiltz told us.

But new developments are taking place. New Ross now has a winery specializing in fruit wines and cider. Muwin Estate Wines began production in 2011 using locally grown blueberries, apples, and other fruit. It now exports as far as China.

And it has a strange forest of thirty-four-foot-tall silver stocks with three thirty-foot petals—a power-generating wind farm called

South Canoe. This $200 million project, located a few miles east of New Ross just off the New Russell Road, will generate enough electricity for thirty-two thousand homes. The turbines were manufactured in Spain and the towers in Stellarton, Nova Scotia.

But the indomitable spirit of William and Mary Ross continues. Four citizens of New Ross, Rubina Hutt, Tina Connors, Jamie Warr, and Scott Hamlin, sat down in a New Ross restaurant and decided there was need of a community plan to counteract the loss of young people—to change the pattern. The New Ross Regional Development Society was formed with a series of strategic goals: to increase business, visitors, and community vitality; retain present businesses; and expand partnerships and community assets. This work is only beginning.

Meanwhile Evelyn Hiltz is enjoying her new life in the century-old house where she grew up. "I get involved; I volunteer at the school, get involved in the church, the historical society writing the newsletter, the committee preparing for the two hundredth anniversary of the founding of New Ross."

This event will commemorate the August walk in of Captain Ross and his 172 disbanded soldiers and the beginnings of this two-century-old community. It will also celebrate the origins of the resulting Ross Farm Museum and its new Learning Centre, now one of the largest employers in town, providing employment for upwards of thirty farm managers and workers, guides, and interpreters. And once again the Ross legacy is manifested in economic as well as cultural terms.

Captain William Ross would be proud.

CHAPTER SEVEN

THE TWENTY-FIRST-CENTURY ROSS FARM MUSEUM

CANADA'S ONLY WORKING FARM-BASED MUSEUM entered the millennium with plans for a major expansion of its facility and mandate. Those plans hinged on a new Learning Centre that would educate students and visitors in traditional farming methods and rural-based life.

The impetus behind the centre was Valerie White, a direct descendant of Capt. William Ross and his wife, Mary, and chair of the board of directors of Ross Farm Museum. "I want us to bring people from different countries to learn basic farming methods and heritage crafts—to become a world leader in redeveloping and fostering these enduring skills," she says.

The Learning Centre can provide programs not possible in the previous restricted space. (MURRAY CREED)

One of the objectives of the board of trustees and the Learning Centre architect, Harry Jost, was to design a building that blended into the centuries-old farmstead and did not overpower Rosebank Cottage and the weathered outbuildings.

This was achieved by constructing a barn-like structure into the hillside, with much of it underground. It would have artifact storage and display space, an expanded gift shop featuring Nova Scotia crafts, generous public meeting facilities, including a commercial kitchen and office, plus improved working space for staff and volunteers.

A year of fundraising produced the funds, originally projected at $3.6 million. The project received $1.25 million each from the Government of Canada and the Province of Nova Scotia, and $100,000 from the municipality of Chester. Another $1.5 million was raised by a twenty-member fundraising cabinet, chaired by Jim Eisenhauer of Lunenburg with honorary co-chairs John Bragg and John Risley. Corporate and private donations came from the New Ross area and all over the province. Every member of Ross Farm Museum board and staff contributed.

In true Ross Farm fashion, the groundbreaking of the new Learning Centre took place using a plow and a team of oxen rather than the traditional shiny shovels. The politicians enjoyed this learning experience, taking turns holding the plow handle while the ox driver led his team and the plow sheer bit into the sod, leaving a straight black row as in the Stan Rogers ballad.

The last cut of hay in the field where the new building and parking lot would sit was harvested using oxen power. Hard hats took over from straw hats as construction began in 2015. Avondale Construction worked through the winter, and by spring a modern reinforced concrete-boned building with a barn-red wood exterior and an interior finished in pine sheathing took shape. It provided no hint of its sophisticated geothermal heating and cooling that employs the heat of the deep earth to keep it warm in winter and cool in summer.

The opening was on May 7, 2016, three months shy of exactly two centuries after Captain William Ross first set foot on that land.

Lisa Wolfe, managing director since 2000, says:

> The new Learning Centre has allowed us to connect more with our community by having exhibitions that tap into our local talent. Pedlars gift shop presents creations from solely Nova Scotian crafters. My hope for the future is that we can create a cottage industry in rural Nova Scotia in crafts and heritage skills and continue to contribute to the economic growth of our rural areas.

Valerie White, who grew up in Rosebank Cottage just down the lane, has high expectations:

> There is a new awakening in young people who want to farm, grow and produce their own food, create heritage crafts such as rug hooking and quilt making, and learn other skills such as barrel making and wrought iron work. We will also work with the community and others to create social enterprise businesses and income to people living in the community.
>
> I believe Captain William Ross and Mary, looking down on what progress has been made, would be very proud to see that their labour has resulted in residents of New Ross and others being proud of their heritage.
>
> I am sure Mary would be thrilled that her precious cottage, Rosebank, has been preserved, and Captain William Ross would see that his commitment to Lord Dalhousie to settle and grow the community has been fulfilled.

Visitors get to see how the original inhabitants of Ross Farm lived. (MATTHEW GATES)

ACKNOWLEDGEMENTS

To Vernon Keddy, current president of the New Ross Historical Society, for access to file cabinets full of documents and antique photos accumulated from many years of research. To Joan Waldron, formerly of the Nova Scotia Museum, for her personal research into the Ross family story in England and Ireland. To Jeanne Howell, Cambridge Military Library, Halifax, for detailed British Army records and housing and living conditions in South and North America, British Army forts in the early 1800s. To Paul O'Brian, Irish National Library, Cork, for details of life and work in that city at that time. To Dan Conlin, Maritime Museum of the Atlantic; Ralph Getson, Fisheries Museum of the Atlantic, Lunenburg; and the Irish High Commissioner of Light, Dublin, for details and background on North Atlantic sailing voyages, navigation, and shipwrecks. To the staff of the Nova Scotia Archives for assistance in unearthing documents and microfilm records, including Edward's diaries; and to Debora Trask, museum curator, for guidance in interpreting these diaries.

ROSS FARM MUSEUM: For first-hand recollections and documents: To the late Ron Barkhouse, first president of the New Ross Museum Society, J. Lynton Martin, retired director of Nova Scotia Museums, who with Allan Hiltz, first director of Ross Farm Museum turned a rundown farm into Canada's only living farm museum.

MUSEUM CURENT OPERATION: To the staff and directors of the museum in the present day, in particular, Valerie White, president of the board of trustees and Lisa Wolfe, managing director, for detailed current information, support, and encouragement. To the late Bob Hutt and to Matthew Gates for present-day Ross Farm photographs, and special thanks to Ernest Cadegan for his inspiring lamb-ewe cover photo, "Taking Instructions."

BOOK RESEARCH AND PRODUCTION: To Whitney Moran, managing editor, Nimbus Publishing, who recognized the value of the story and guided the shaping of the manuscript to the format of the series, and Elaine McCluskey, who saw this book through to publication.

BIBLIOGRAPHY

DesBrisay, Judge Mather B. *History of Lunenburg County.* Originally published by William Briggs, Toronto, 1895.

Hanson, Sharon. *Rose Bank Cottage.* MG Audiobook Pub.

Leopold, Caroline Broome. *The History of New Ross in the County of Lunenburg, Nova Scotia.* (Published for the Committee in Charge, 150th Anniversary of New Ross, 1966, Middleton, Nova Scotia: Black Print. Co.)

Martell, J. S. *Stage Coaches in Nova Scotia.* The Collections of the Nova Scotia Historical Society.

Martin, J. Lynton. *The Ross Farm Story, Farm Life in Western Nova Scotia prior to 1850.* Nova Scotia Museum, 1986.

Maurice, Maj. Gen. Sir F. *The 16th Foot–A History of The Bedfordshire and Hertfordshire Regiment.* Published by Constable and Co., 1931

Trask, Deborah. Transcriptions of the *Diaries of Edward Ross*, and related papers .e.g. *The Edward Ross Diaries.*

Royal Nova Scotia Society Journal. *Military Settlements in Nova Scotia after the War of 1912.*

ARCHIVAL MATERIAL

Evans; *General and Field Officers 1807*, British Army listings; *Officers of the Army and Royal Marines on full and half-pay.*

1812 War – Famous Regiments, Lt. Gen. Sir Brian Horrocks War Office, 1814.

New Ross Historical Society files gathered by Ronald Barkhouse and his successor, Vernon Keddy.

NEWSPAPERS

The Wexford Recorder, Ireland. Report of Shipwreck on Tuskar Rock.

The Edinburgh Annual Register, Scotland. Report of shipwreck on Tuskar Rock.

The Acadian Recorder, Halifax. Report of William Ross's death and burial.

INDEX

Numbers set in italics refer to images.

S

T

V

W

Y

Other Books in this Series

STORIES OF OUR PAST

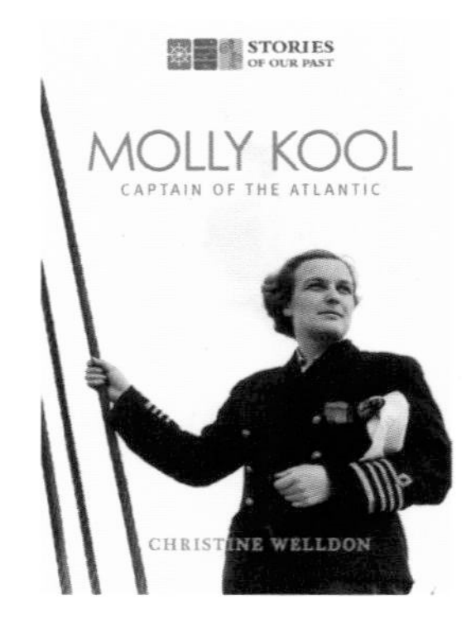

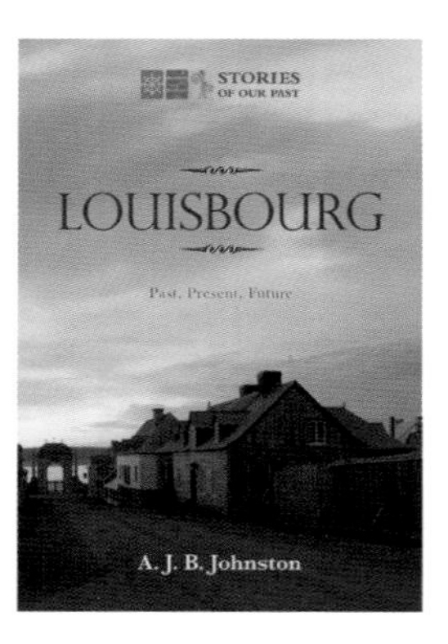

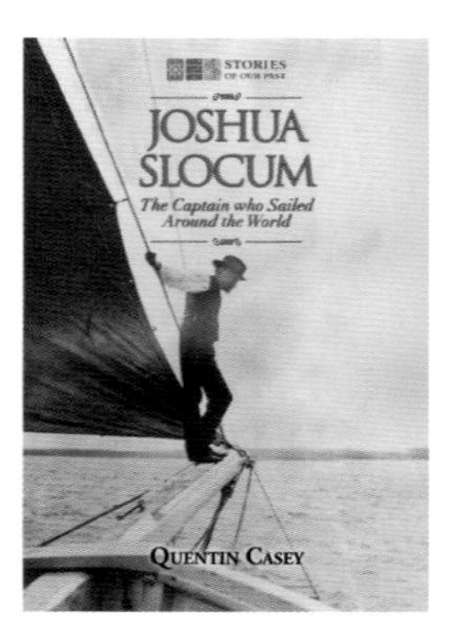

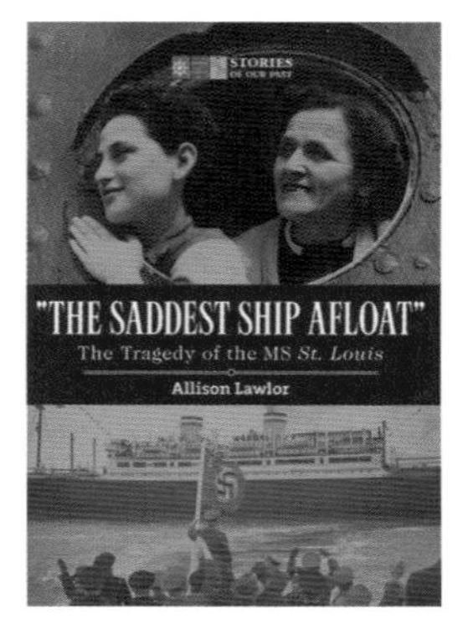

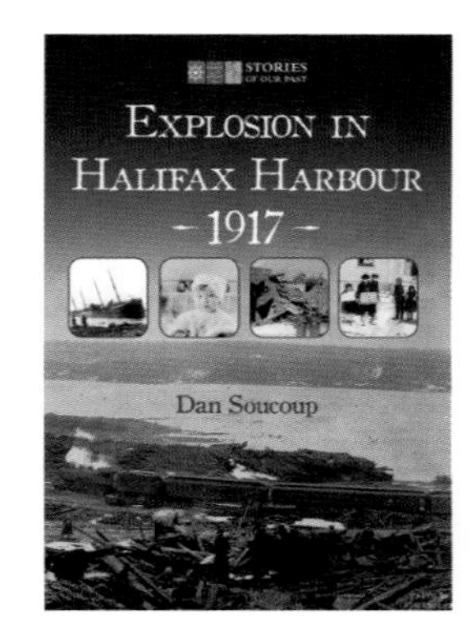